P9-DEU-228

THE
Holistic Herbal
DIRECTORY

THE
Holistic Herbal
DIRECTORY

A DIRECTORY OF HERBAL REMEDIES
FOR EVERYDAY HEALTH PROBLEMS

PENELOPE ODY

CHARTWELL
BOOKS, INC.

First published in 2001 by
CHARTWELL BOOKS INC.
A Division of Book Sales Inc.
114 Northfield Avenue
Edison, New Jersey 08837

ISBN: 0-7858-1351-9

Copyright © The Ivy Press Limited 2001

The moral right of the author to be identified as
the author of this work has been asserted by her in accordance
with the Copyright, Designs, and Patents Act of 1988.

All rights reserved. No part of this publication may be
reproduced in any material form (including photocopying or
storing it in any medium by electronic means and whether
or not transiently or incidentally to some other use
of this publication) without the written permission
of the copyright owner.

Note from the publisher
Information given in this book is not intended to be
taken as a replacement for medical advice. Any person with
a condition requiring medical attention should consult
a qualified medical practitioner or therapist.

This book was conceived, designed,
and produced by
THE IVY PRESS LIMITED
The Old Candlemakers
West Street
Lewes, East Sussex BN7 2NZ

Publisher: SOPHIE COLLINS
Art Director: CLARE BARBER
Designer: KEREN TURNER, JANE LANAWAY
Editor: MANDY GREENFIELD
DTP Designer: CHRIS LANAWAY
Herb illustrations: PAULINE ALLEN
Montage illustrations: PIP ADAMS
Mac illustrations: RICHARD CONSTABLE
3D models: MARK JAMIESON
Studio photography: WALTER GARDINER PHOTOGRAPHY,
IAN PARSONS, GUY RYECART
Picture research: VANESSA FLETCHER

Originated and printed in China

Contents

How this book works

Holistic medicine is all about treating the whole person, focusing not just on physical symptoms but on emotional and spiritual aspects contributing to the disorder. This is the approach that has always been taken by herbalists—be they trained in traditional Western methods, Chinese medicine, or ayurveda. The *Holistic Herbal Directory* adopts the same definition of the term "holistic," but also looks at how each of these traditional therapies would tackle a particular ailment, to give a comprehensive approach to therapy.

Below *In holistic traditions there is both a spiritual and a mental aspect to maintaining and restoring good health.*

The directory starts with an explanation of the basic concepts of herbal medicine in the Western, Chinese, and ayurvedic traditions, and how they differ in the way they use herbs—orthodox Western medicine tends to relieve rather than cure the symptoms of illness, whereas in the herbal tradition, both East and West, emphasis is placed on harmony and balance of body and mind, with herbs used in combination. An A–Z of herbs and an A–Z of common ailments provide useful cross-references to the different herb names in Western, Chinese, and ayurvedic traditions and to the illnesses they may help. These are followed by advice on how to make up simple herbal remedies, ranging from infusions, tinctures, and syrups to Chinese decoctions and various ayurvedic remedies.

Each tabbed section takes a different system of the body and outlines your treament options for certain ailments. A carefully

Above *Introductions to each herbal tradition explain the differences in approach between them.*

Below *Descriptions of the ailments are followed by details of the herbs that may help to ease them.*

balanced approach ensures that Western, Chinese, and ayurvedic options are described throughout, together with the herbal remedies. Within each herb profile, the parts of the plant used, its taste, character, the meridians that it affects, and its actions (defined in the glossary on pp.202–3) are all described. These are followed by a detailed outline of the herb's principal uses, together with a note on any cautions of which you should be aware. The term "cautions" is used in this book also to refer to any contra-indications (that is, any factor in a patient's condition which indicates that a remedy involves a greater-than-normal degree of risk and which it is therefore unwise to pursue). In Chinese medicine, cautions are often as expressed as "avoid if there is no sign of X or Y" or "take only if there is X or Y," referring to a prevailing condition.

The book ends with details of how to assemble your own herbal first-aid kit, a glossary of terms used throughout the book, and useful addresses of suppliers and herbal organizations.

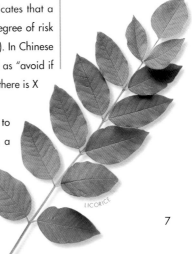

LICORICE

7

Western medicine and herbs

BASIL

Western orthodox medicine as we know it today is a comparatively recent invention of the past 30 years. Until the end of the seventeenth century medical practice was still based on the theories of the ancient Greeks and was named "Galenic" medicine in memory of the famous second-century Roman physician Claudius Galenus.

HIPPOCRATES AND HUMOURS

The Greeks believed that everything was made from four fundamental elements—earth, air, fire, and water. The nature of these elements influenced the seasons and all living things, and they were characterized by "basic qualities": heat or cold, dryness or moisture. The elements also controlled four vital bodily "humors" and ancient doctors argued that human health depended on keeping these humors—"blood," "phlegm," "yellow bile," and "black bile"—in balance.

These beliefs date back to at least 600 BC and the earliest Greek philosophers. By the time of Hippocrates (c. 468–377 BC), who is now known as the "father of medicine," they were well established. Hippocrates related illness to the pattern of changing seasons influenced by the elements and recommended that certain foods and herbs were used at particular times of year—much as Chinese Taoists had done in their rather different, five-element model *(see p.15)*. The herbs that Hippocrates used were a mixture of native and imported plants, absorbing ideas from Assyria and India (with Eastern herbs such as basil and ginger among the most prized), as well as European and North African species, the use of which can be dated back in Egyptian papyri to around 1700 BC.

Below The ancient Greek physician Hippocrates was revered in his day for his understanding of sickness and health.

Early physicians were often priests and healing was as much a matter of pacifying evil spirits as prescribing curative brews. This is a connection still found in many traditional cultures, where the shaman or medicine man combines incantations, herbs, and trance states in an attempt to visit the spirit world and persuade whatever is troubling the patient to depart.

Following Hippocrates, it was Galen (see box) who became the most influential medical practitioner in the Western world, but with the fall of Rome in the fifth century, the center of classical learning shifted east and the study of Galenic medicine became focused on Constantinople and Persia. In the Arab world Galenism was enthusiastically adopted at the time of the prophet Muhammad and merged with folk beliefs and surviving Egyptian traditions kept alive by the Copts. The great Arab scholars added to Galen's original work and it was the resulting mixture of herbal ideas and traditions that was reimported into Europe with the Arab armies that invaded Spain in the eleventh to twelfth centuries. Probably the most important work of the time was the *Kitab al-Qanun*, or *Canon of Medicine*, by Avicenna (Abdallah Ibn Sina, born at Bokhara in c. 980). This was based firmly on Galenic principles and by the twelfth century had been translated into Latin and become one of the most important medical textbooks.

The Arabs added many exotic herbs and spices from the East to the European *materia medica*. Nutmeg, cloves, and saffron were introduced by Arab physicians, while Chinese rhubarb entered Europe via the Arab trade routes.

GALEN

Claudius Galenus (AD 131–199) was a physician from Pergamum in Asia Minor, who had trained in Alexandria, was court physician to the emperor Marcus Aurelius, and was known as Galen to later generations. He reworked many of the old Hippocratic ideas and formalized the theories of humors. He was a prolific writer and his books became classical medical texts, not only of the Roman world but of medieval Europe and of the Arabic medicine that survives in much of the Muslim world today.

Below *Nutmeg is one of several spices introduced from the East to the West by Arab physicians.*

A BALANCED VIEW OF HEALTH

For at least 2,000 years European medicine was dominated by these ancient Greek ideas. The humors were regulated by various drastic treatments: bleeding the patient to remove a surfeit of blood, giving strong purgatives to clear excess black bile, or emetics to regulate phlegm and yellow bile. The humors were believed to be largely responsible not only for health and disease, but also for human emotions and personalities. Depression and unhappiness, for example, were associated with the "melancholic" temperament where black bile was dominant; to improve the mood it was believed necessary to "purge" the black bile with remedies that today we would describe as strong laxatives, such as figs or licorice.

As late as 1650 William Harvey (1578–1657), who first demonstrated the circulation of the blood, was still following Galenic principles in his prescribing. One of his surviving remedies is for John Aubrey (1626–97), author of *Brief Lives*, and uses senna *(Senna alexandrina)* and rhubarb together with Christmas rose or hellebore *(Helleborus niger)* in order to purge black bile.

Like the elements, the humors were also related to temperature and degree of dryness and could be balanced by herbs that had the opposite characteristics. Phlegm was, understandably, cold and damp, so herbs that were hot and dry —such as elder flowers—might be used to clear a productive cough or watery catarrh. Thyme and hyssop are also in the hot and dry category and were prescribed for the sort of phlegmatic excess

Above *In Galenic theory different temperaments were linked to personality and to probable illnesses associated with the four humors.*

Below *Elder flowers are a warm, dry herb used to treat cold and damp.*

that one encounters in the common cold. Galen's descriptions of herbs along the lines of "hot in the third degree" or "cold in the second" remained in use well into the eighteenth century.

Today, Galenic theories continue to dominate medicine in much of the Islamic world, where they are known as *Tibb* or *Unani*, and they also linger in our own common terminology: "phlegmatic" individuals still correspond to Galen's original description, while "sanguine" people are usually confident optimists—with the same characteristics that the early Greeks ascribed to those people in whom "blood" dominated.

Above *Hyssop is a hot, dry herb and is useful for respiratory problems.*

SCIENCE TAKES THE LEAD

As the seventeenth- and eighteenth-century researchers gradually discovered human physiology and began to take a more scientific approach to the causes of disease, so the Galenic theories gradually fell into disrepute—and with them many traditional herbal remedies. Instead doctors now preferred the newer drugs. At first many of these were based on toxic minerals, but later chemicals were extracted from the old herbs and were synthesized *(see box)*.

Below *The drug aspirin was originally synthesized from willow bark, an old remedy for gout and fever.*

THE DEVELOPMENT OF MODERN DRUGS

Morphine was first identified in 1803 in Germany by Friedrich Wilhelm Adam Sertürner (1783–1841), who succeeded in extracting a white crystalline compound from crude opium poppy. Before long, similar techniques had produced aconitine from monkshood, emetine from ipecacuanha, atropine from deadly nightshade, and quinine from Peruvian bark. By 1850 salicin —identified as one of the active ingredients in willow bark—had been synthesized and a modified form was launched by the German pharmaceutical company Bayer in 1899 as aspirin, the first modern patent drug.

Today many of our most important pharmaceutical drugs can be traced back to herbs, frequently used in much the same way since the days of Galen. However, extracted chemicals are often extremely potent and can cause effects that were unknown when the whole plant was used. Many herbs actually contain ingredients that mediate potential side effects—meadowsweet contains mucilaginous substances to protect the lining of the stomach and prevent the plant's salicin-like compound from damaging the mucous membranes. With no such protective mucilage, excess aspirin is a well-known cause of gastric ulceration. In its transition from crude plants to clinical pills, modern medicine has lost not only the simplicity of using whole plants (with their chemical ingredients to reduce the risk of side effects), but also the art of combining herbs to modify their toxicity, which survives in traditional Chinese herbalism.

Above *Meadowsweet has similar properties to willow bark.*

Below *While modern medicine views the human body mechanistically, the Chinese system sets great store by the meridians that channel Qi energy.*

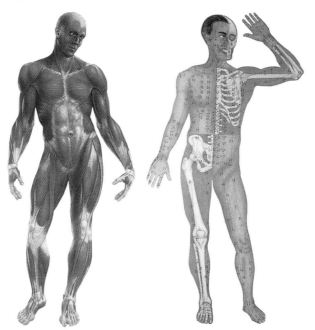

The use of herbal derivatives in modern medicine also tends to be very different from the herbalist's approach. Traditional healers used their remedies to help the body overcome illness—to strengthen what some termed the "vital force": an energy concept similar to *Qi* or *prana*. Herbs would work with the body to strengthen tissues and restore humoral balance.

Modern pharmaceutical drugs, in contrast, are designed primarily to relieve symptoms. To the traditional healer, symptoms are important as they give clues to what is wrong; if drugs remove the symptoms, then treating the disease can be more difficult. Taking pain-killers to relieve an aching back does not cure what is causing the pain; it just gets rid of the discomfort.

Above *Western pharmacists still make extensive use of herbs in many of their medicinal preparations.*

Below *Modern drugs aim to relieve symptoms, rather than restore the patient to health.*

13

Traditional Chinese Medicine and herbs

SHAN ZHA

Chinese herbal medicine dates back to at least the year 2500 BC, when the mythical figures of the Yellow Emperor (Huang Di) and the Divine Farmer (Shen Nong) laid down its basic concepts and first classified medicinal herbs.

MAINTAINING BALANCE

Like early Greek science, the traditional Chinese "world view" regarded everything as made up of basic elements: in this case there were five—earth, metal, water, wood, and fire—which control all things, including our bodily well-being and "balance."

Chinese medicine of 2500 BC was closely linked with religion: Shen Nong and Huang Di were Taoists, and many early Chinese herbals and medicinal texts (such as the *Huang Di Nei Jing Su Wên*, or *Yellow*

Below In Chinese theory the five elements are linked in a complex pattern of generation and control.

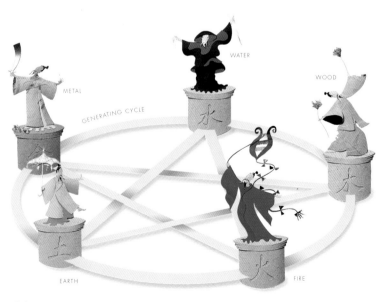

METAL

GENERATING CYCLE

WATER

WOOD

EARTH

FIRE

Emperor's Canon of Internal Medicine) are also rich in Taoist spiritual wisdom. Taoism is a way of life that concentrates on achieving prosperity, longevity, and even immortality through "virtue"—which, to its followers, means conformity to nature, both within the individual and beyond. Herbs, especially potent tonics such as *Ling Zhi* and ginseng, were regarded as helping to strengthen this adherence to virtue and thus leading to a long life and good fortune.

The five elements are related to each other and to all things, so that an imbalance in one particular element may lead to an overexuberance or weakness of the elements that it is said to control or support. The five elements are also related to five solid *(Zang)* organs and five hollow *(Fu)* organs or "bowels," which similarly interact with one another. A weakness in the wood element (associated with the liver), for example, may lead to "deficient fire" (heart), while earth (spleen), which is controlled by wood, would become overdominant and thus lead to a depletion of water energy (kidney).

Above *The Yellow Emperor of Chinese mythology passed on his knowledge in the form of a classic medicinal text.*

Taoism also lays great store on opposites, arguing that beauty exists only because there is ugliness, good because there is evil. This in turn gave rise to the theory of *Yin* and *Yang*, which is also important in Traditional Chinese Medicine (TCM). *Yang* and *Yin* are seen as two aspects of the whole: light and dark, male and female, hot and cold, and so on. These same forces affect human health and each of the five bodily organs of the five-element model, which need to be kept in balance. Too much *Yang* and the organ is overstimulated, overheated, and prone to dryness; too much *Yin* and a cold, damp disease syndrome can result.

Below *The principles of* Yin *and* Yang *are opposites, such as night and day, winter and summer, cold and hot, moist and dry.*

FIVE-ELEMENT ASSOCIATIONS

	Wood	Fire	Earth	Metal	Water
DIRECTION	East	South	Center	West	North
COLOR	Green	Red	Yellow	White	Black
SEASON	Spring	Summer	Late Summer (traditionally from c. 7 July for 1 month)	Fall	Winter
CLIMATE	Wind	Hot	Dampness	Dryness	Cold
SOLID ORGAN *Zang*	Liver	Heart	Spleen	Lung	Kidney
HOLLOW ORGAN *Fu*	Gall bladder	Small intestine	Stomach	Large intestine	Urinary bladder
SENSE ORGANS /OPENINGS	Eyes Sight	Tongue Speech	Mouth Taste	Nose Smell	Ears Hearing
EMOTION	Anger	Joy/fright	Worry	Sadness/ grief	Fear
TASTE	Sour	Bitter	Sweet	Pungent/acrid	Salty
TISSUES	Tendons Nails	Blood vessels Complexion	Muscles Lips	Skin Body hair	Bone Head hair
SOUND	Shouting	Laughing	Singing	Weeping	Groaning
SMELL	Rancid	Burnt	Fragrant	Rotten	Putrid
BODY FLUID	Tears	Sweat	Saliva	Mucus	Urine
MEAT	Chicken	Mutton	Beef	Horse	Pork
CEREAL	Wheat	Glutinous millet	Millet	Rice	Beans

As well as the body organs, Chinese medicine talks of basic "life materials" or "fundamental substances." These concepts are very different from our Western view of physical entities.

QI or "vital energy" comes into this category and has become a familiar term in the West. There are many sorts of *Qi*, each with a specific function or associated with a certain organ; for instance, *Wei Qi*, or defense *Qi*, which equates roughly to the Western concept of the immune system. The other four concepts are perhaps less familiar to Western readers:

JING or "essence" is the most important fundamental substance—the source of living organisms. It is stored in the kidney and can be congenital (derived from our parents and with us from birth) or acquired (produced by the spleen from food, air, and water). Congenital essence decays during our life and cannot be replaced. Its loss is blamed for the physical signs of aging.

XUE or "blood" is seen as a mixture of nourishing *Qi*, food essence, and body fluids. It can be regarded on one level as no more than the blood circulating in our veins and arteries, but is also essential for mental activities: if *Xue* and *Qi* are strong, then a person will be clear-thinking and vigorous.

JIN-YE are body fluids—*Jin* indicates the clear aspect of fluid, while *Ye* suggests a turbid (thick) component. Among the *Jin-Ye* are saliva, gastric juices, phlegm, tears, mucus, and sweat. Both *Xue* and *Jin-Ye* are regarded as predominantly *Yin* in nature, so any illness involving dryness might be seen as involving *Yin* deficiency.

SHEN or "spirit" is the inner strength behind both essence and energy, and is closely associated with human consciousness. If *Shen* is damaged in any way, then a person may be forgetful, slow-thinking, suffer from insomnia or—in extreme cases—be violent.

Above Ren Shen, *or ginseng, is used to strengthen* Qi.

Above *Walnut, or* Huo Ta Ren, *strengthens* Jing, *vital essence.*

Above Ling Zhi, *the reishi mushroom, is used to strengthen* Shen, *or spirit.*

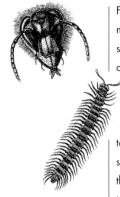

For the Chinese, illness is not a matter of invading micro-organisms, diseased or damaged tissues, or stress-related problems. Illness is defined more in terms of inner balance between *Yin* and *Yang*, the strength of vital energy *(Qi)* or essence *(Jing)*, and harmony between the *Zang-Fu* organs. "Superficial" syndromes, such as colds or muscular aches and pains, are likely to be blamed on invading "evils": wind, heat (or summer heat), cold, fire, dampness, and dryness. If these superficial or external problems are inadequately treated, then the "evils" may invade the interior, leading to more chronic health problems.

Above *Centipedes and other insect material such as hornets' nests are sometimes used in Chinese medicine.*

HERBS IN CHINESE MEDICINE

To the Chinese, the term "herbs" does not suggest just the fruits, leaves, barks, roots, and seeds of Western herbalism, but also includes an array of minerals, insects, and animal parts that most Westerners find rather unsavory. This has marred the reputation of Chinese medicine in the West in recent years. Even more confusing for Westerners, the same "drug" can be derived from a number of different botanical species, depending on where in China it is collected. Medicinal plants include many that are closely related to Western species, such as dandelion and elecampane, as well as those plants we would consider ornamental, such as magnolia, forsythia, and buddleia.

Below *Different parts of the same plant often go under different names on packaging, and the labels change again if the dried plant is stir-fried or treated with ginger before use.*

The properties of these various herbs are matched to the five-element model, with plants being ascribed particular tastes and energies. They can be hot, warm, neutral, cool, or cold, while taste matches the

classic five tastes of pungent, sweet, sour, bitter, and salty, plus two further options—astringent or bland/neutral. Herbs are also defined in terms of the *Zang-Fu* organs which they affect by "entering" the specific acupuncture meridian associated with that organ. These meridians comprise a network of energy channels where *Qi* flows just below the surface of the body.

CHINESE PRESCRIPTIONS

It is rare for a Chinese prescription to comprise only one or two herbs—usually four or more are combined, in a traditional formula that often dates back to the earliest practitioners. During their training Chinese medical students learn many thousands of these formulae by heart, each one a specific remedy for an exactly defined disease syndrome. Within the prescription each herb also has a precise role *(see box)*.

Above *Dandelion leaves are used as a diuretic in the West, while the Chinese use them to clear heat and toxins from the blood.*

THE ROLE OF THE HERBS

EMPEROR *The principal therapeutic herbs*

MINISTER *Herbs that support and strengthen the key plants*

MESSENGER *Herbs whose directional properties "target" the prescription to particular meridians or parts of the body*

HELPER OR HARMONIZER *Auxiliary and/or correcting herbs, which can counter any toxic effects of the major ingredients or deal with secondary symptoms in the condition*

The prescriptions may be used as a standard remedy or modified to suit the individual. In the West, some of the most popular combinations are available prepacked in tablets or as powdered mixtures; these are often supplied by acupuncturists as a convenient remedy. Herbalists generally prefer to blend the raw herbs, adjusting the mixture to suit the patient.

Ayurvedic medicine and herbs

Traditional Indian medicine is usually termed ayurvedic, from *ayur* (meaning life) and *veda* (meaning knowledge). It is a "knowledge of how to live," accurately reflecting the fact that good health is the responsibility of the individual.

Above *In Ayurvedic treatment gemstones can be used for their therapeutic effects.*

EARLY BEGINNINGS

Ayurvedic medicine has its roots in the original Dravidian culture of India (c. 5000 BC), while the earliest surviving literature—the *Rig Veda*, dating from around 2500 BC—includes information on surgery and the use of prostheses, and lists 67 medicinal herbs.

The basic medical theories of ayurveda were extended and codified during the first and second centuries AD, with the Middle Ages bringing new medicines in the form of minerals and metal-based drugs. By the sixteenth century Mogul and European invaders had introduced Western ideas (initially in the form of Greek Galenic medicine, which was known to the Muslims as *Tibb* or *Unani*) and ayurveda went into decline. Pressure for Indian independence in the 1920s, however, brought about a revival of many

Below *An Indian sage addresses an attentive king and his court on wisdom.*

PITTA

VATA

KAPHA

traditional practices and today ayurvedic medicine is being taught alongside Western theory in many Indian universities. The Islamic teachings also survive, with a flourishing tradition of *hakims—Unani* doctors—spreading around the world with immigrants from Pakistan and Bangladesh. There are currently believed to be around 250,000 ayurvedic practitioners in India alone, ranging from university-trained medics to traditional healers.

THE BASICS OF AYURVEDA

Like traditional Galenic medicine, ayurvedic health care is about keeping the humors in balance—in this case there are three of them *(tri doshas)*: *pitta* (bile, linked to the fire element), *vata* (wind, associated with the air and ether elements) and *kapha* (phlegm or dampness, ruled by the elements of water and earth).

Also vital is *prana*—the inner life force—which ayurvedic practitioners feel at a pulse. The life force gives rise to fire: the fire of digestion and mental energy; *prana* is also linked to breath or oxygen, which feeds the fire. If the fire is weak, then the body is likewise weak.

This inner fire is called *agni* or *tejas*, while the relationship between *prana* and *tejas* gives rise to *ojas*, or good digestion, and thus health. This good digestion is equated with juice or sap, which in turn produces the six experiences or tastes that are so crucial in ayurvedic herbalism. The three humors can also be

Above Pitta *or bile is linked to the fire element; vata or wind is linked to air and ether; kapha or phlegm is linked to water and earth.*

PITTA

VATA

KAPHA

Above *The names of the* tri doshas—pitta, vata, *and* kapha—*as they are written in Sanskrit.*

21

seen as the waste products of the digestion process—the end product of the *prana-tejas-ojas* interaction. The more imperfect the digestion, the more waste products *(ama)* there are and the more imbalances there will be in the system.

However, as with Traditional Chinese Medicine, philosophy and medical theory are closely intertwined. There are the cosmic forces—*prana*, the breath of life; *agni*, the spirit of light or fire; and *soma*, a manifestation of harmony, cohesiveness, and love. Early Sanskrit writings regarded creation as a continuous interchange between the two basic principles: *praktri* (unconscious nature or energy) and *purusha* (consciousness or matter), rather like modern theories of quantum mechanics.

Purusha is further subdivided into the three essential qualities, or *gunas*: *sattva*, which can be translated as cognition or clarity; *rajas*, or action; and *tamas*, which is desire or substance. These three qualities give rise to the three psychic forces: *buddhi* (intellect); *ahamkara* (ego); and *manas* (mind or spirit). For good health, balance is also needed among the three *gunas*. *Sattva* is regarded as purity and enlightenment, while *rajas* and *tamas* are the dark side of nature (distraction and dullness respectively). All three, however, are needed and spiritual health is maintained by learning to control *rajas* and *tamas* while developing the calm clarity of *sattva*.

Below *The three essential qualities of matter, or* gunas, *are known as* sattva *(clarity or enlightenment) and the two dark sides of nature:* rajas *(distraction) and* tamas *(dullness).*

PLASMA

BLOOD

MUSCLE

FAT

BONE

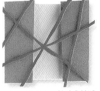

MARROW AND NERVE TISSUE

SEMEN

Healthy balance also requires the seven *dhatus*, or tissues, to be in equilibrium. These are: plasma *(rasa)*, blood *(rakta)*, muscle *(mamsa)*, fat *(medas)*, bone *(asthi)*, marrow and nerve tissue *(majja)*, and semen *(shukra)*. There are also *srotas*, or "channels," that must be open, allowing breath, food, and water to flow freely into and around the body. These include familiar organs (the esophagus, trachea, veins, arteries, and intestines), but the *srotas* can also be compared with the Chinese acupuncture "meridians," which allow energy to flow around the body. There are also the three waste products or *malas* (urine, sweat, and feces), which need to be in balance. *Agni*, the life force (or more prosaically, the digestive function) also needs to be strong. Food, drink, sensual gratification, light, fresh air, and spiritual activities all "feed" *agni*, helping to maintain the balance of the *tri doshas* and ensure correct functioning of *dhatus, malas,* and *srotas*.

Above *The seven types of tissue* (dhatus) *have to be kept in balance.*

Below *The* srotas *of ayurvedic tradition are similar to the Chinese acupuncture meridians.*

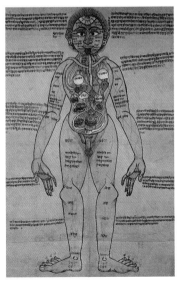

'There is nothing in the
universe which cannot be
used as a medicine

No root which is
not a medicine

No word that is
not a mantra

No human being
who is not useful.'

AYURVEDIC SAYING

HERBS IN AYURVEDA

Around 800 herbs are used in the "great tradition" of ayurvedic medicine, although throughout India some 2,500 medicinal herbs are used. Each household has its *maharastra*, or "grandmother's purse," filled with healing herbs for the household. Many of these herbs, such as sandalwood, turmeric, and saffron, are very familiar in the West. Others, such as *bhringaraj*, are used in ways that are similar to Chinese tradition.

As in Chinese medicine, combinations of herbs are generally used in preference to simples, with many traditional medicated jellies, pastilles, and pills being widely available. Indian pharmaceutical companies are also researching herbal remedies for the orthodox-medicine market. Herbs are often taken in *ghee* (clarified butter) or milk to increase their tonic effects and there is extensive use of medicated oils, which are believed to be especially effective in strengthening specific *dhatus* and *agni*.

Right *Ayurvedic remedies may be prepared as pills or capsules ready for use.*

AYURVEDIC HERBS TEND TO BE CLASSIFIED BY BROAD RANGE OF ACTION, INCLUDING

- *Alterative (cleansing) herbs*—rakta shodhana karma
- *Anthelmintic (anti-parasitic) herbs*—krumighna karma
- *Astringent (tissue-constricting) herbs*—stambhana karma
- *Carminative herbs (expel gas)*—vata anuloman
- *Diaphoretic (sweat-promoting) herbs*—svedana karma
- *Diuretic (urine-promoting) herbs*—mutrala karma
- *Emmenagogues (menstruation-promoting herbs)*—raktabhisarana karma
- *Expectorant herbs (encourage the coughing reflex)*—kasa svasahara
- *Laxative herbs (promote defecation)*—virechana karma
- *Stimulant (arousing) herbs*—dipana pachana karma
- *Tonics (strengthening and enlivening agents)*—bruhana karma *(nutritive tonics)*, rasayana karma *(rejuvenative tonics)*, and vajikarana *(aphrodisiacs)*.

AYURVEDIC TASTES

In ayurveda a balanced diet is not one that contains the right vitamins, proteins, and so on, but one that includes the right proportions of the six tastes or *rasas*: sweet, sour, salty, pungent, bitter, and astringent. Each taste corresponds to a pair of elements (with one dominating) and is classified in terms of heating or cooling, whether it is heavy or light, and the degree of dampness and dryness. The tastes can variously weaken or strengthen the corresponding *doshas* and are used to counter specific weaknesses and fulfil particular bodily functions. The sweet taste, for example, promotes growth. It also stimulates the digestion and seems to strengthen the first or root *chakra* (energy center) at the base of the spine—sweet herbs are used for threatened abortion or to strengthen the memory. Bitter herbs and foods help to reduce excess *pitta* and *kapha* and detoxify the system. They are used for fevers or skin conditions.

Above *A liking for sweet things indicates an affinity to the earth or the water element and the emotion of desire.*

TASTES, ELEMENTS, AND EMOTIONS
The six tastes affect different body systems. The elements and groups of emotions are also assigned to the tastes. Excess of these emotions can have a similar effect to eating too much of a particular taste.

TASTES	ELEMENTS	TYPES OF EMOTIONS
Sweet	Earth/water	Desire
Salty	Water/fire	Greed
Sour	Earth/fire	Envy
Astringent	Earth/air	Fear
Pungent	Air/fire	Anger
Bitter	Air/ether	Grief

Below *Asafetida, or hingu, is a pungent herb that is used to clear food stagnation.*

A–Z of herbs

BOTANICAL NAME followed by page reference		WESTERN	CHINESE Mandarin	AYURVEDIC Sanskrit/Hindi
Achillea millefolium	133	Yarrow	I Chi Kao	gandana
Acorus calamus	51	Sweet flag	Shi Chang	puvacha
Aesculus hippocastanum	139	Horse-chestnut	-	-
Agrimonia eupatoria	192	Agrimony	-	-
Agrimonia pilosa	192	-	Xian He Cao	-
Alchemilla xanthoclora	173	Lady's-mantle	-	-
Alisma plantago-aquatica	167	Water-plantain	Ze Xie	-
Allium sativum	128	Garlic	Da Suan	rashona
Aloe spp.	63	Aloe vera	Lu Hui	kumari
Alpinia galanga	133	Galangal	-	kulanjian
Alpinia officinarum	133	-	Gao Liang Jiang	-
Althaea officinalis	78	Marshmallow	-	-
Angelica polyphorma var. sinensis	173	Chinese angelica	Dang Gui	-
Angelica pubescens	153	Pubescent angelica	Du Huo	-
Apium graveolens	150	Celery	-	-
Arctium lappa	67	Burdock	Niu Bang	-
Arnica montana	146	Arnica	-	-
Artemisia absinthum	97	Wormwood	-	-
Artemisia vulgaris	112	Mugwort	Ai Ye	nagadamani
Asparagus racemosus	105	Asian asparagus	Tian Men Dong	shatavari
Astragalus membranaceus	105	-	Huang Qi	-
Atractylodes chinensis	91	-	Cang Zhu	-
Atractylodes macrocephala	78	-	Bai Zhu	-
Avena sativa	109	Oats	-	-
Azadirachta indica	67	Neem	-	nimba
Berberis aristata	84	-	-	daru haridra
Berberis vulgaris	84	Barberry	-	-
Bupleurum falcatum	84	-	Chai Hu	-
Calendula officinalis	63	Marigold	-	-
Cannabis sativa	88	Marijuana	Huo Ma Ren	-
Capsicum frutescens	128	Tabasco pepper	-	marishi-phalum
Carthamus tinctorius	129	Safflower	Hong Hua	-
Caulophyllum thalictroides	187	Blue cohosh	-	-
Centella asiatica	106	Indian pennywort	-	gotu kola
Chamaelirium luteum	178	-	-	-
Chamaemelum nobile	192	Roman camomile	-	-
Chionanthus virginicus	85	Fringetree	-	-
Cimicifuga racemosa	178	Snakeroot	-	-
Cinnamomum camphora	157	Camphor	Zhang Nao	karpura
Cinnamomum cassia	129	Cinnamon	Gui Zhi	twak
Citrus reticulata	41	Tangerine	Chen Pi	-
Codonopsis pilosula	119	-	Dang Shen	-
Coix lachryma-jobi	167	Job's tears	Yi Yi Ren	-
Commiphora molmol	49	Myrrh	Mo Yao	bola
Commiphora mukul	119	Guggul	-	guggula
Cornus officinalis	164	Dogwood	Shan Zhu Yu	-
Corydalis solida	147	-	Yan Hu Suo	-
Crataegus laevigata	137	Hawthorn	-	-
Crataegus monogyna	137	Hawthorn	-	-

BOTANICAL NAME followed by page reference		WESTERN	CHINESE Mandarin	AYURVEDIC Sanskrit/Hindi
Crataegus pinnatifida	137	Hawthorn	Shan Zha	-
Crocus sativus	181	Saffron	Fan Hong Hua	nagakeshara
Curcuma longa	130	Turmeric	Jiang Huang	haridra
Cyperus rotundus	174	Nutgrass	Xiang Fu	-
Dendranthema x grandiflorum	64	Chrysanthemum	Ju Hua	
Dimocarpus longan	120	Longan	Long Yan Rou	-
Dioscorea opposita	79	-	Shan Yao	-
Dioscorea villosa	79	Atlantic yam	-	-
Echinacea angustifolia	45	Echinacea	-	-
Echinacea pallida	45	Echinacea	-	-
Echinacea purpurea	45	Echinacea	-	-
Eclipta prostata	70	-	Han Lian Cao	bhringaraj
Elettaria cardamomum	93	Cardamom	-	ela
Eleutherococcus senticosus	109	Siberian ginseng	Wu Jia Pi	-
Emblica officinalis	64	Emblic myrobalan	-	amalaki
Ephedra sinensis	47	Ephedra	Ma Huang	somalata
Equisetum arvense	184	Horse-tail	-	-
Eschscholzia californica	197	California-poppy	-	-
Eucalyptus globulus	197	Eucalyptus	-	-
Eucommia ulmoides	164	-	Du Zhong	-
Eupatorium perfoliatum	195	Boneset	-	-
Euphorbia hirta	47	Pill-bearing spurge	-	nagarjuni
Euphrasia officinalis	65	Eyebright	-	-
Fagopyrum esculentum	130	Buckwheat	-	-
Ferula assa-foetida	95	Asafetida	E Wei	hingu
Filipendula ulmaria	184	Meadowsweet	-	-
Foeniculum vulgare	65	Fennel	Xiao Hui Xiang	shatapushpa
Forsythia suspensa	57	Forsythia	Lian Qiao	-
Fucus vesiculosis	150	Bladderwrack	Kun Bu	-
Galium aparine	57	Bedstraw	-	-
Ganoderma lucidem	117	Reishi mushroom	Ling Zhi	-
Ginkgo biloba	120	Ginkgo	Bai Guo	-
Glycyrrhiza glabra	41	Licorice	-	yashti madhu
Glycyrrhiza uralensis	41	-	Gan Cao	-
Hamamelis virginianum	155	Witch-hazel	-	-
Harpagophytum procumbens	151	Devil's claw	-	-
Humulus lupulus	115	Hops	-	-
Hypericum perforatum	111	St.-John's-wort	-	-
Hyssopus officinalis	42	Hyssop	-	-
Inula brittanica	42	-	Xuan Fu Hua	-
Inula grantioides	42	-	-	pushkaramula
Inula helenium	42	Elecampane	-	-
Inula racemosa	42	-	-	pushkaramula
Juglans regia	165	Walnut	Hu Tao Ren	-
Laminaria spp.	150	Kelp	Kun Bu	
Lamium album	170	White deadnettle	-	
Lavandula angustifolia	141	Lavender	-	

ECHINACEA

BOTANICAL NAME followed by page reference		WESTERN	CHINESE Mandarin	AYURVEDIC Sanskrit/Hindi
Leonurus cardiaca	134	Motherwort	-	-
Leonurus heterophylus	134	-	*Yi Mu Cao*	-
Ligusticum wallichii	174	Szechuan lovage	*Chuan Xiong*	-
Ligustrum lucidum	121	Glossy privet	*Nu Zhen Zi*	-
Lonicera japonica	45	Honeysuckle	*Jin Yin*	-
Lycium barbarum	85	Lycii	*Gou Qi Zi*	-
Lycium chinense	85	Chinese wolfberry	*Gou Qi Zi*	-
Matricaria recutita	192	German camomile	-	-
Melaleuca alternifolia	195	Tea tree	-	-
Melilotus officinale	139	Melilot	-	-
Melissa officinalis	111	Lemon-balm	-	-
Mentha arvensis	79	Field mint	*Bo He*	-
Mentha x piperita	79	Peppermint	-	-
Morus alba	198	White mulberry	*Sang*	-
Morus nigra	198	Black mulberry	-	-
Myristica fragrans	91	Nutmeg	*Rou Dou Kou*	*jatiphala*
Nelumbo nucifera	80	Lotus	*Lian*	*padma*
Nepeta cataria	198	Catmint	-	-
Ocimum basilicum	117	Basil	-	-
Ocimum sanctum	117	Sacred basil	-	*tulsi*
Oenothera biennis	68	Evening-primrose	-	-
Ophiopogon japonicus	134	Dwarf lily-turf	*Mai Men Dong*	
Paeonia lactiflora	86	White peony	*Bai Shao Yao*	
Paeonia lactiflora	68	Red peony	*Chi Shao Yao*	
Paeonia suffruticosa	175	Tree peony	*Mu Dan Pi*	
Panax ginseng	106	Ginseng	*Ren Shen*	
Panax quinquefolius	107	American ginseng	*Xi Yang Shen*	-
Passiflora incarnata	115	Passion-flower	-	-
Petroselinum crispum	168	Parsley	-	-
Phellodendron chinense	69	Chinese corktree	*Huang Bai*	-
Piper nigrum	80	Black pepper	*Hu Jiao*	*marich*
Plantago ovata	89	Isphagula	-	*snigdhajira*
Plantago psyllium	89	Psyllium	-	*snigdhajira*
Platycodon grandiflorus	43	Balloonflower	*Jie Geng*	-
Polygonum multiflorum	179	Fleeceflower	*He Shou Wu*	-
Prunella vulgaris	199	Self-heal	*Xia Ku Cao*	-
Prunus persica	131	Peach	*Tao Ren*	-
Psoralea corylifolia	165	-	*Bu Gu Zi*	-
Pulsatilla vulgaris	187	Pasque-flower	-	-
Rehmannia glutinosa	53	Prepared Chinese foxglove	*Shu Di Huang*	
Rehmannia glutinosa	53	Raw Chinese foxglove	*Sheng Di Huang*	-
Rheum palmatum	89	Rhubarb	*Da Huang*	*amla vetasa*
Rosa canina	113	Dog rose	-	-
Rosa damascena	113	Damask rose	-	*shatapatri*
Rosa laevigata	113	Cherokee rose	*Jin Ying Zi*	-
Rosa rugosa	113	Japanese rose	*Mei Gui Hua*	-
Rosmarinus officinalis	71	Rosemary	-	-
Rubus chingii	185	-	*Fu Pen Zi*	-

SAGE

BOTANICAL NAME followed by page reference		WESTERN	CHINESE Mandarin	AYURVEDIC Sanskrit/Hindi
Rubus idaeus	185	Raspberry	-	-
Rumex crispus	151	Curly dock	-	-
Salix alba	153	White willow	-	-
Salvia miltiorhiza	135	Chinese sage	*Dan Shen*	-
Salvia officinalis	49	Sage	-	-
Sambucus nigra	55	Elder	-	-
Santalum alba	81	Sandalwood	-	*chandana*
Schisandra chinensis	181	Chinese magnolia-vine	*Wu Wei Zi*	-
Scutellaria baicalensis	137	Baikal skullcap	*Huang Qin*	-
Scutellaria lateriflora	103	Blue skullcap	-	-
Serenoa repens	171	Saw palmetto	-	-
Sida cordifolia	155	-	-	*bala*
Silybum marianum	86	Milk-thistle	-	-
Stachys officinalis	121	Betony	-	-
Stellaria media	69	Chickweed	-	-
Symphytum officinale	147	Comfrey	-	-
Syzygium aromaticum	156	Cloves	*Ding Xiang*	*lavanga*
Tabebuia impetiginosa	95	-	-	-
Tanacetum parthenium	141	Feverfew	-	-
Taraxacum mongolicum	87	-	*Pu Gong Ying*	-
Taraxacum officinale	87	Dandelion	-	-
Terminalia belerica	51	Bekeric myrobalan	-	*bibhitaki*
Terminalia chebula	51	Chebulic myrobalan	*He Zi*	*haritaki*
Thymus vulgaris	43	Thyme	-	-
Tilia cordata	193	Linden	-	-
Tribulis terrestris	168	-	*Ci Ji Li*	*gokshura*
Trifolium pratense	179	Red clover	-	-
Trigonella foenum-graecum	81	Fenugreek	*Hu Lu Ba*	*methi*
Turnera diffusa var. *aphrodisiaca*	171	Damiana	-	-
Ulmus rubra	93	Slippery elm	-	-
Urtica dioica	71	Stinging nettle	-	-
Vaccinium myrtillus	97	Bilberry	-	-
Vaccinium oxycoccus	169	Small cranberry	-	-
Valeriana officinalis	103	Valerian	-	*tagara*
Verbascum thapsus	53	Mullein	-	-
Verbena officinalis	87	Vervain	*Ma Bian Cao*	-
Viola tricolor	193	Johnny-jump-up	-	-
Vitex agnus-castus	175	Chaste-tree	-	-
Vitex rotundifolia	175	-	*Man Jing Zi*	-
Withania somnifera	107	-	-	*ashwagandha*
Wolfiporia cocos	169	-	*Fu Ling*	-
Xanthium sibiricum	55	-	*Cang Er Zi*	-
Zea mays	199	Cornsilk	*Yu Mi Xu*	-
Zingiber officinale	185	Ginger	*Jiang*	*adraka*
Zizyphus jujuba	131	Chinese-date	*Da Zao*	-
Zizyphus jujuba var. *spinosa*	135	Wild date seeds	*Suan Zao Ren*	-

RASPBERRIES

A–Z of common ailments

GARLIC

How to make simple herbal remedies

DRIED STINGING NETTLE

Making simple herbal remedies at home need be no more difficult or time-consuming than brewing a cup of tea. More complex herbal products, such as ointments and creams, are now readily available from health-food stores and pharmacies, so this section focuses only on the simpler options.

INFUSIONS

The aerial parts of herbs (leaves, flowers, and stems) can easily be made into teas or tisanes by infusing them in water. The usual Western approach is to use 1oz/25g of dried herb to 1pt/500ml of water that is just off the boil. Infuse the mix for ten minutes, then strain and drink in three equal wine-glass or cup doses during the day. The infusion should be stored in a pitcher, covered, in a cool place and used within 24 hours. Alternatively, use 1–2tsp of the dried herb per cup and make a dose at a time. If using fresh herbs, three times as much plant material (i.e. 3oz/75g) is needed. For cold infusions, see macerations below.

Below *Making a herbal infusion is as easy as making a cup of tea.*

DECOCTIONS

Herbal roots, berries, and barks need to be made into decoctions to extract the active ingredients. The usual Western dose is 1oz/25g of dried root to 1½pt/750ml of water, simmered in a stainless-steel or enamel saucepan until the volume has reduced by about one-third, then strained. Store in a pitcher in a cool place and use in three wine-glass doses during the day, reheating it if preferred. Decoctions may be flavored with a little honey.

TINCTURES

A tincture is an alcoholic extract of the active ingredients in a herb, made by soaking the dried or fresh plant material in a mixture of alcohol and water for two weeks and then straining the mix through a wine press or jelly bag. Commercially produced tinctures are usually made from ethyl alcohol. In some countries this is readily available duty-free, but in others the supply is strictly controlled by the authorities: vodka makes a suitable alternative as it contains fewer other flavorings than most alcohol. Standard herbal tinctures usually contain 25 percent alcohol in water (i.e. 1fl oz/25ml of pure alcohol with 3fl oz/75ml of water). This is a little weaker than most commercial spirits (usually 37.5 percent alcohol), so the vodka will need diluting with water (1½pt/750ml of vodka to ¾pt/375ml of water) to make the required strength.

Above *Ingredients such as juniper berries and gentian root are generally made into decoctions.*

Put 8oz/200g of the dried herb into a large jar and pour over 1½pt/750ml of the alcohol/water mixture. If using fresh herbs, then you need to use three times as much (i.e. 1½lb/600g of fresh herb to 1½pt/750ml of liquid). Store in a cool place for two weeks, shaking the mixture each day, then filter through a wine press or cheesecloth bag. Store the tincture in clean, dark glass containers. Tinctures will last for two years or more without deterioration, although ayurvedic medicine argues that they increase in potency with age.

Below *A maceration is strained through a piece of cheesecloth after being left to stand overnight.*

MACERATIONS

Some herbs, such as valerian and marshmallow root, are best macerated in cold water. Use the same proportions as for an infusion and simply leave the mixture in a cool place overnight. In the morning, strain the mixture and use as an infusion.

Above *Marshmallow leaves are used in infusions, while the root is macerated in herbal preparations.*

SYRUPS

Sugar or honey will act as a preservative for herbal infusions and decoctions, while the sweetness can be very soothing for coughs. Make a standard infusion or decoction, then strain the mixture and add 1lb/500g of unrefined sugar or honey to each 1pt/500ml of liquid. Stir this in a cast-iron or stainless-steel saucepan over the heat until the sugar or honey is completely dissolved and the mixture forms a syrup. Allow to cool and then store in clean glass bottles closed with a cork. Do not use screw-tops—syrups often ferment and tight lids will lead to exploding bottles.

CHINESE DECOCTIONS

Chinese remedies are generally dispensed by practitioners in separate bags containing enough dried herb for each dose. This is traditionally boiled in three cups of water in an earthenware or ceramic pot for 25–30 minutes until the liquid has reduced by half. The mix is then strained and taken in a single dose on an empty stomach in the morning. Sometimes the herbs need to be reheated in fresh water and then the two extractions are combined.

The same herbs might be used for the following day's brew, depending on the exact mix: if it contains soluble ingredients, such as certain mineral salts, then a fresh prescription will be needed each day. The decoction—known as *Tang* (soup)—is generally extremely dark brown and very strongly flavored. Chinese doses are much larger than those used by Western herbalists—often up to 3½oz/90g—and the resulting mix is usually rather unpleasant for Western palates.

Above *Brown sugar or honey is used to make syrups from herbal infusions and decoctions.*

TONIC WINES

A daily glass of tonic wine is a delightful way to take herbal remedies. A crockery vinegar vat is best, although a large rum pot or glass jar is also suitable. Fill the vat with the chosen tonic herb—ideally using a root remedy such as ginger, licorice, or *Dang Gui* rather than leafy parts—then cover with a good-quality red wine (preferably organic). Leave the mix for at least two weeks before drawing the liquid off in a daily sherry-glass dose (2–3fl oz/60–75ml). Keep the herb covered with more red wine to prevent it from going moldy. The wine will continue to extract active constituents from the roots for several months before you need to replace the herbs.

Above *Herbal teas can be taken in the elegant Chinese way, sipped from china bowls.*

Below *The dried root of Dang Gui, or Chinese angelica, is a popular tonic herb.*

35

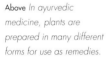

AYURVEDIC REMEDIES

Traditionally ayurvedic remedies are taken as fresh juices, pastes, or purées, generally mixed with *ghee* or oil; as decoctions; as hot and cold infusions; or as macerations. The traditional proportion for decoctions is one part herb to 16 parts water, which is then simmered until the volume has reduced to one-quarter of the original. This process takes several hours to complete. Hot infusions use the proportion of one part herb to eight parts boiling water, with the infusion being left for up to 12 hours, rather than the 10–15 minutes that are generally allowed in the West.

Some ayurvedic practitioners in the West recommend increasing the dosage and cutting the simmering or infusion time to Western proportions in order to make the preparation more compatible with Western lifestyles. Decoctions can be simmered until three-quarters of the water is left and dosages doubled or trebled, with a similar increase in dosages for a minimum hot-infusion time of 30 minutes.

Milk decoctions are made from one part herb to eight parts milk and 32 parts water. They are then simmered until all the water has evaporated. Using herbal powders with milk and omitting all the water is another shortcut that can be made.

Above *In ayurvedic medicine, plants are prepared in many different forms for use as remedies.*

Right *In a decoction, the herbal ingredients are simmered for a long time before the resulting liquid is strained.*

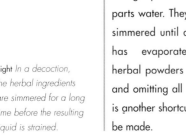

RESPIRATORY SYSTEM
Western Approach

Orthodox Western medicine views the lungs and airways as an efficient gas-exchange system, drawing air into the body, extracting the oxygen (which is carried away in the bloodstream), and excreting surplus carbon dioxide and water that are produced by the body's metabolic processes.

Below *Environmental pollution is the cause of many respiratory problems.*

Air travels through the nasal passages into the trachea or windpipe, passing through the larynx, where its movement sets up the necessary vibrations that enable us to speak. It moves onward through a network of bronchi, bronchioles, and alveoli to ensure that as much air is exposed to as many blood vessels as possible to allow the vital gaseous exchange to take place.

In mechanistic terms, respiratory disorders are associated with blockages in the airways: infections causing inflammation, and pollutants or allergens causing irritation, which may lead to excess mucus production, phlegm, and catarrh. Orthodox treatments center on antibiotics to combat micro-organisms or on expectorants to encourage coughing and expel phlegm.

Below *Thyme is a hot, dry herb that is useful for clearing chest infections.*

Traditional Western (Galenic) medicine regarded the lungs as damp in character. They were closely associated with the phlegmatic humor, so any excess would be characterized by watery catarrh, while deficiency would lead to dryness with harsh coughs. Hot, dry herbs were used to treat excess conditions and cold, damp ones to combat deficiency. A more holistic Western approach links the lungs and breath to tension: deep breathing exercises are now recognized as an important component in relaxation.

Above *Breathing exercises can be practised to strengthen the lungs.*

Above *The calligraphy for "lungs" (Fei).*

In Traditional Chinese Medicine the lung is classified among the *Zang* (solid) organs and, although held to be responsible for respiration, it also has an important role in maintaining the circulation of *Qi* (vital energy) and the clear fluids and water produced in digestion.

As with all the organs, Chinese theory links additional attributes, including emotions and a spiritual aspect, with the lung: it is associated with grief and is believed to store vitality or "animal energy" *(Po)*. The lung's health is said to be "seen in the skin and body hair"—healthy, glowing skin indicates strong lung *Qi*; it is also, not surprisingly, linked to the nose—a red, sore nose is, after all, unpleasantly familiar among those suffering from colds and catarrh.

The association with *Qi* is also logical since breath, which enters via the lungs, can be seen as an energizing force, with traditional exercise routines being designed to improve breath control. Among them is *Qigong*, a practice becoming more familiar in the West, which literally means "breathing exercise."

The lung is particularly associated with the type of energy called "defense *Qi*" *(Wei Qi)*, which it directs to the body's surface to repel invading "evils" that may cause imbalance and ill health. Colds and flu can thus be seen as the lung's inability to combat external "evils."

The lung's own intrinsic *Qi* moves downward in the body, so coughs producing mucus and phlegm (productive coughs) are often regarded as a sign of "rebellious lung *Qi*" *(Fei Qi Shang Ni)* moving in the wrong direction. They are treated with herbs designed to reverse the flow. Ailments such as pleurisy are defined in terms of weak lung *Qi*.

Right *The plant* Acorus calamus *is a cleansing remedy used in ayurvedic medicine to treat sore throats.*

Below *Suffering from throat infections can be a sign that* kapha *is dominant.*

Ayurvedic medicine sees the lungs (and the stomach) as being dominated by the water humor *(kapha),* so respiratory problems are generally associated with a surfeit of this. Individuals where *kapha* dominates are thus more likely to suffer from colds, catarrh, throat infections, asthma, and similar disorders. *Kapha* is also linked with digestion, so an excess of mucus and catarrh may indicate weak digestive energy *(agni)* and a failure to metabolize foods correctly. Respiratory disorders may be treated with remedies designed to strengthen *agni* and clear internal dampness. In severe cases, this can involve the use of herbal emetics to cause vomiting and purge stomach phlegm.

Kapha problems manifest with thin, copious, watery catarrh and frothy sputum, rather than the thicker, yellow varieties that are linked to heat and the *pitta* humor (fire). Excess *pitta* is associated with the sorts of lung problems that Western medicine would blame on invading bacteria, such as colds, acute bronchitis, and some types of pneumonia.

As in TCM, the lungs are also closely associated with air—seen as the life force, or *prana*—which is strengthened in many yoga exercises. Shortness of breath and wasting diseases (such as tuberculosis) are therefore defined as an imbalance in the *vata* (air) humor. Treatment involves not only herbs and massage oils but also *pranayama* (breathing exercises). In these, exhalation should be twice the length of the in-breath, with alternate nostril breathing often used: in through the right nostril, out through the left for excess *kapha* conditions, with the opposite for *pitta* problems.

OTHER HERBS THAT MAY BE HELPFUL
pill-bearing spurge (p.47) ● *marshmallow (p.78)* ● *slippery elm (p.93)*
● *asafetida (p.95)* ● *comfrey (p.147)* ● *eucalyptus (p.197)*

COMFREY

Coughs

Coughing is the body's natural response to any blockage of the airway. That might include dust and traffic fumes or mucus resulting from infection. Coughing can also be a symptom of more serious illness, so professional medical attention is needed for any cough that persists for more than a few days or where there is no obvious cause.

Western herbal medicine uses a range of remedies for coughs: some encourage the production of phlegm, while others act as cough suppressants. These are often combined with anti-microbials to combat infection or with tonic herbs to help strengthen the lungs.

Chinese medicine often uses similar plants, but these tend to be defined as "directional" remedies that will send lung **Qi** downward or generally improve **Qi** circulation. Catarrh and phlegm are associated with excess heat and dampness—pneumonia, bronchitis, and similar congestive problems are seen as phlegm-heat blocking the lung and interfering with the normal **Qi** flow. Many traditional cough remedies are also now known to be strongly antibacterial and expectorant.

Ayurvedic remedies are usually either anti-pitta, in order to clear excess heat from the system, or more drying if the problem is associated with too much kapha or watery catarrh.

PHLEGM

Coughs can be dry and irritating or productive, with phlegm that can vary in shade from white to green. Colored phlegm generally indicates an infection and, if it is streaked with blood, then professional medical help is required.

CITRUS RETICULATA   Tangerine/*Chen Pi*

PARTS USED *peel* TASTE *pungent, bitter* CHARACTER *warm* MERIDIANS *lung, spleen, stomach* ACTIONS *anti-asthmatic, anti-inflammatory, carminative, digestive stimulant, expectorant, circulatory stimulant; trials have also shown that the plant is effective for acute mastitis*

USES The peel of both ripe tangerines (*Chen Pi*) and unripe (*Qing Pi*) is used in Chinese medicine. *Qing Pi* focuses more on the liver and gall bladder, while *Chen Pi* is used to strengthen and move stagnant spleen and stomach *Qi*, dry dampness, resolve phlegm, and reverse the upward flow of *Qi* in productive coughs. It is useful as a carminative to ease abdominal discomfort and poor appetite, and as an expectorant for coughs with copious sputum. In Chinese terms, vomiting is related to rising *Qi*, so *Chen Pi* is used to combat nausea. CAUTIONS: Avoid in hemoptysis and if there is no sign of damp/phlegm stagnation.

GLYCYRRHIZA SPP.   Licorice/*Gan Cao*/*yashti madhu*

PARTS USED *root* TASTE *sweet* CHARACTER *neutral* MERIDIANS *heart, lung, spleen, stomach* ACTIONS *anti-bacterial, anti-inflammatory, antispasmodic, anti-allergenic, antitussive, hypotensive, steroidal action, cholagogue*

USES As well as strengthening *Qi*, *Gan Cao* (*G.uralensis*) is used to clear heat, moisten the lungs, and stop coughing. In the West a related species (*G. glabra*) is used for digestive and respiratory problems, for gastric ulcers, and constipation. In India the plant is known as *yashti madhu*, or honey stick, and is mainly used to increase *kapha*, lubricate the lungs, and liquefy mucus. It is often used with ginger for colds with coughs. CAUTIONS Avoid *Gan Cao* in abdominal fullness; avoid licorice in excess *kapha* syndromes or high blood pressure; best avoided in osteoporosis.

HYSSOPUS OFFICINALIS Hyssop

PARTS USED *leaves* TASTE *pungent, bitter*
CHARACTER *dry, neutral* MERIDIANS *lung, spleen, large
intestine* ACTIONS *expectorant, carminative, peripheral
vasodilator, diaphoretic, anticatarrhal, topically anti-
inflammatory, antiviral* (Herpes simplex)

....

USES Like other members of the mint family, hyssop is a
bitter digestive tonic and useful in cooking, but its main
medical application is for the upper respiratory tract: it
is ideal for infections, bronchial congestion, coughs,
and feverish chills. It helps to strengthen and energize
Yang and some Western herbalists compare it in action
to *Jie Geng* (see p.43). As a digestive remedy it can
be useful for wind and colic and is quite safe to use
with children. The essential oil is mildly sedative and
can be added to relaxing baths.

CAUTIONS Excessive use of the essential oil may cause
convulsions.

INULA SPP. Elecampane/*Xuan Fu Hua*/*pushkaramula*

PARTS USED *root/flower heads* TASTE *salty, pungent*
CHARACTER *warm* MERIDIANS *lung, spleen, stomach,
large intestine* ACTIONS *elecampane—tonic, stimulating
expectorant, diaphoretic, antibacterial, antifungal, antiparasitic; Xuan Fu Hua—antibacterial, nerve stimulant,
digestive stimulant*

....

USES The root of the European species (*I. helenium*) is
an effective expectorant and tonic—a useful restorative
after flu. The Chinese prefer the flowers of *I. brittanica*
(*Xuan Fu Hua*) to redirect upwardly flowing lung and
stomach *Qi* and clear stagnant phlegm from the lungs
in bronchitis. In ayurveda *pushkaramula* (*I. racemosa* or
I. grantioides) is used as a lung tonic, mainly in asthma.
It is often used in combination with other heating herbs,
such as cinnamon, ginger, and long pepper.

CAUTIONS None noted.

PLATYCODON GRANDIFLORUS   Balloonflower/*Jie Geng*

PARTS USED *root* TASTE *pungent, bitter* CHARACTER *neutral* MERIDIANS *lung* ACTIONS *antifungal, antibacterial, expectorant, hypoglycemic, reduces cholesterol levels*

USES *Jie Geng* is traditionally used in Chinese medicine in order to circulate lung *Qi* and clear excess phlegm associated with external wind, cold, and heat problems. It also helps to clear pus from abscesses and is used for sore throats and hoarseness. It is combined with mulberry leaves (*Sang Ye*), chrysanthemum flowers (*Ju Hua*), field mint (*Bo He*), and licorice (*Gan Cao*) in a traditional mixture called *Sang Ju Yin*, which is given for coughs and colds. In Western terms *Jie Geng* would be classified as an expectorant for productive coughs with profuse phlegm that are often associated with infections.

CAUTIONS Avoid in tuberculosis.

THYMUS VULGARIS   Thyme

PARTS USED *aerial parts* TASTE *pungent* CHARACTER *hot and dry* MERIDIANS *lung, spleen* ACTIONS *antiseptic, expectorant, antispasmodic, astringent, antimicrobial, diuretic, antitussive, antibiotic, wound healer, topically rubefacient*

USES Like many culinary herbs, thyme is a good digestive remedy, helping the system to cope with rich foods and reducing wind and flatulence. It is extremely antiseptic and a good expectorant—ideal for clearing phlegm and combating chest infections. Traditionally it was classified as "hot and dry in the third degree," making it a very potent remedy for damp or phlegmatic conditions. The essential oil is also stimulating and tonic and can be added to relaxing baths or to rubs, for muscular aches, pains, and stiffness.

CAUTIONS None noted.

OTHER HERBS THAT MAY BE HELPFUL
elder (p.55) ● *sage (p.49)* ● *myrrh (p.49)* ● *guggul (p.119)*
● *peppermint (p.79)* ● *Huang Qi (p.105)* ● *ginger (p.185)*
● *catmint (p.198)* ● *elecampane (p.42)* ● *boneset (p.195)*

SPINACH LEAVES

Colds and flu

In the West common colds and influenza
are usually blamed on viruses, and Western
herbal treatment focuses on antiviral remedies.

Before the discovery of viruses, earlier generations

blamed an assortment of "venoms" or magical "evils" for sudden

colds and this is similar to the traditional Chinese approach, where the

six "external evils" of cold, heat or "summer heat," fire, wind, damp, and

dryness are seen as the prime causes of superficial or "external"

diseases. These "evils" are more successful when the Wei Qi (defense Qi)

is weak. Common colds are generally blamed on "wind-cold" or "wind-

heat evils," with chilliness and an absence of sweating suggesting a

"cold" problem, while fever and thirst

indicate a "heat" problem. Warming or

cooling herbs are used as appropriate.

In ayurveda the common cold is usually

associated with a surfeit of kapha

(phlegm), due to seasonal weather or the

result of eating too many kapha-forming

foods. Treatment is through a kapha-

lowering diet with plenty of whole grains

VIRUSES

Viruses are micro-organisms
which frequently mutate and
are spread in droplets of
moisture when we sneeze,
causing the familiar variety
of "cold" symptoms—
nasal catarrh, sore throats,
sneezing, aching limbs—as
our bodies struggle to combat
the infection.

and steamed vegetables, supported by warm, spicy herbs to encourage

sweating. Occasionally excess pitta or vata is blamed—as with the Chinese

concept of wind-heat—and then cooling, moistening remedies are chosen.

ECHINACEA SPP. Echinacea

PARTS USED *roots of all three species, plus aerial parts of* E. purpurea **TASTE** *pungent* **CHARACTER** *cool, dry* **MERIDIANS** *lung, large intestine* **ACTIONS** *antibiotic, immune stimulant, anti-allergic, lymphatic tonic, anti-inflammatory, diaphoretic, wound healer*

USES An important anti-infection remedy extensively studied in Europe since the 1930s, echinacea *(E. angustifolia, E. purpurea, and E. pallida)* is known to stimulate the immune system in some (as yet unknown) way to combat invading bacteria, fungi, and viruses. It is ideal for almost any common infection—including colds, flu, and urinary-tract infections—and has also been used in AIDS therapy. Although the root is more commonly used, recent German research suggests that the aerial parts of *E. purpurea* may be just as effective.

CAUTIONS High doses may occasionally cause nausea and dizziness.

LONICERA JAPONICA Honeysuckle/*Jin Yin*

PARTS USED *flower buds, stems* **TASTE** *sweet* **CHARACTER** *cold* **MERIDIANS** *lung, stomach, large intestine* **ACTIONS** *antibacterial, hypotensive, anti-inflammatory, mild diuretic, antispasmodic*

USES Honeysuckle flowers *(Jin Yin Hua)* are used in China for colds and fevers attributed to "wind-heat;" it also clears the toxins or "fire poisons" that TCM regards as causing such conditions as boils and dysentery. It is a very cold remedy, used in high fevers, and is sometimes fried to reduce its cold nature and extend its range of use. Like the flowers, the stems *(Jin Yin Teng)* treat feverish colds and dysentery, but are also used to remove heat from the channels by stimulating the circulation of *Qi*. They are strongly cooling and are used, with other herbs, for acute rheumatoid arthritis.

CAUTIONS Avoid in cold conditions.

OTHER HERBS THAT MAY BE HELPFUL
elecampane (p.42) ● *ginseng (p.106)* ● *eyebright (p.65)*
● *elder (p.55)* ● *camomile (p.192)* ● *fennel (p.65)*

ELECAMPANE

Asthma and hay fever

Both asthma and hay fever are often associated in the West with allergies. Irritants cause an inflammatory reaction, which in asthma leads to narrowing of the airways and the characteristic wheeze. Hay fever is similarly associated with allergens attacking the mucous membranes of the nasal passages. Western treatment usually includes anti-inflammatories, antispasmodics and anti-allergens.

In ayurveda both disorders are further classified by kapha, vata, or pitta dominance. Asthma is normally kapha-type, with an abundance of phlegm and white sputum; pitta-type has yellow phlegm; and vata-type is likely to be dry, causing excessive thirst. Hay fever is usually vata; the pitta form is likely to be associated with more extensive allergies, and kapha with excess phlegm and watery catarrh. All three types are linked to debility and constitutional weakness.

ASTHMA LINKS

Western theory often associates asthma with an allergic response to dairy products, wheat, and beef, among common allergens; others include car fumes, tobacco smoke, dust mites, and animal fur. Asthma can be severe and life-threatening: it should always be taken seriously.

In TCM the causes of asthma can be rather more complex: the complaint may be due to a failure of kidney energies to coordinate respiration (in which case it would be treated with kidney tonics) or it may be associated with an internal accumulation of "phlegm-heat" or weak lung Qi. All require careful diagnosis and appropriate treatment.

EPHEDRA SINENSIS   Ephedra/*Ma Huang*/*somalata*

PARTS USED *twigs or stems* TASTE *pungent, bitter*
CHARACTER *warm* MERIDIANS *lung, urinary bladder*
ACTIONS *antispasmodic, febrifugal, diaphoretic,
diuretic, antibacterial, antiviral*

USES *Ma Huang* is mainly used in China as a diaphoretic to combat "wind-cold" and coughs. It is baked with honey for use as an anti-asthmatic or combined with cinnamon twigs, apricot seeds, and licorice in *Ma Huang Tang*, a popular formula for "wind-cold" problems. It is also occasionally used for kidney disorders. In the West it is better known as the source of the drug ephedrine, often used for nasal congestion and catarrh. Professional herbalists frequently include small doses in asthma remedies.
CAUTIONS Avoid in high blood pressure; use is restricted in some countries.

EUPHORBIA HIRTA   Pill-bearing spurge/*nagarjuni*

PARTS USED *aerial parts* TASTE *pungent* CHARACTER *heating*
MERIDIANS *lung, liver* ACTIONS *anti-asthmatic, antispasmodic,
anticatarrhal, expectorant*

USES Known as "asthma weed" in the West, pill-bearing spurge is a native of India and Australia, where it was traditionally used to treat this complaint. In India, where it is also known as *laldudhi* (Hindi), the whole plant is also given for intestinal worms and kidney disorders; a wash is used for skin sores. The root is anti-emetic. In the Philippines, decoctions were a traditional eye remedy and in Hawaii it was used for poultices and gargles. It is known to relax the bronchioles and ease breathing. In the early part of the twentieth century it was used in anticancer remedies, and some anti-tumor properties have been recorded.
CAUTIONS None noted.

OTHER HERBS THAT MAY BE HELPFUL
echinacea (p.45) ● *agrimony (p.192)* ● *raspberry (p.185)*
● *guggul (p.119)* ● *rosemary (p.71)* ● *marigold (p.63)*

Mouth problems

**Problems of the mouth, such as gum disease and
aphthous ulcers (stomatitis), are usually blamed, in the West, on either
infection or poor diet: excess sugars and poor dental hygiene can create
an environment where fungi and bacteria flourish, leading to an increased
risk of infection. Treatment generally focuses on antimicrobial herbs such
as echinacea.**

In Chinese medicine the mouth is closely linked with the spleen and the
stomach, so any weakness or poor condition in the mouth area is likely
to be seen as a symptom of deficient spleen energy or of inadequate
digestive function.

Other oral conditions are generally blamed on an imbalance occurring
elsewhere in the body: dry mouth and gums, for example, may suggest
that "excess stomach heat" is drying essential body fluids, while bleeding
gums may imply that there is an "upward flaring of stomach
heat." Chinese treatments therefore usually focus on
digestive herbs in order to strengthen and normalize
both the spleen and stomach function.

In ayurveda bleeding gums and mouth
inflammations are similarly linked to heat—in this
case to excess pitta. Remedies usually feature either
astringent or cooling herbs, such as myrrh, while

SESAME SEEDS sesame oil is routinely rubbed into the gums in order to

strengthen the tissue in this area.

COMMIPHORA MOLMOL   Myrrh/*Mo Yao*/*bola*

PARTS USED *gum resin* TASTE *bitter, astringent*
CHARACTER *neutral, cool* MERIDIANS *heart, liver, spleen*
ACTIONS *antifungal, antiseptic, astringent, immune stimulant, bitter, expectorant, circulatory stimulant, anticatarrhal*

USES Myrrh resin is collected as a thick, pale-yellow liquid from the cut stems of the bush. It dries to a reddish-brown solid, which is then dissolved in tinctures and oils. Myrrh is a highly astringent herb used to stop bleeding from wounds or gums and ease sore throats and mouth ulcers. It is antimicrobial, so it is helpful for infections. In ayurveda it is used to prevent decay and reverse the aging process and is rejuvenative for *kapha* and *vata*. In China it is used as a painkiller to "move stagnant blood," and to promote wound healing.

CAUTIONS Avoid in pregnancy.

SALVIA OFFICINALIS   Sage

PARTS USED *leaves* TASTE *pungent, bitter* CHARACTER *cool, drying* MERIDIANS *spleen, lung, kidney* ACTIONS *carminative, antispasmodic, astringent, and healing to the mucous membranes, antiseptic, peripheral vasodilator, suppresses perspiration, reduces salivation and lactation, uterine stimulant, systemically antibiotic, hypoglycemic, bile stimulant, antioxidant*

USES Sage is ideal for healing problems in the mouth and throat. It was often an ingredient in medieval "tooth pastes" and is still found in similar herbal products. It makes an excellent gargle and mouthwash for minor infections and gum inflammation. The plant has a high estrogen content and antioxidant properties, so makes a useful menopausal remedy, and has a deserved reputation for encouraging longevity. Sage ointment is used on minor cuts and insect bites.

CAUTIONS Avoid high doses in pregnancy or epilepsy.

OTHER HERBS THAT MAY BE HELPFUL
sage (p.49) ● *rosemary (p.71)* ● *agrimony (p.192)*
● *raspberry (p.185)* ● *myrrh (p.49)* ● *Lian Qiao (p.57)*

Throat problems

In the West throat problems are usually linked to common

colds and infections causing inflammation of the pharynx

(pharyngitis) or larynx (laryngitis). There is generally dryness,

hoarseness, and difficulty in swallowing. The standard treatment is

antimicrobials to combat the underlying infection and soothing, astringent

herbs to ease the discomfort and inflammation.

In TCM acute sore throats are generally regarded as being due to

invasion by "wind-heat evils," in a similar way to certain types of

common colds. Once these "external evils" move inside the body, they can

lead to a range of more serious ills,
including pneumonia and bronchitis, so
the aim is always to treat such syndromes
while they are still "superficial."

In ayurveda sore throats are
categorized depending on the underlying
humoral imbalance: kapha sore throats
have associated phlegm, while vata sore
throats are dry and are treated with
moist, mucilaginous remedies, such as

VOCAL CORDS
The vocal cords consist of two
membranes lying across the
windpipe.and forming part
of the larynx. Sounds are
created by vibration of the
cords (which are moved by
muscles and cartilage in the
larynx) as the air passes
between them. Strain on the
vocal cords may contribute
to throat problems.

ghee or sweet flag. Pitta conditions are generally linked to infections, so

antimicrobial herbs are used. The throat chakra (energy center) is also

significant, with voice quality and strength being linked to both the

humors and energy levels.

ACORUS CALAMUS   Sweet flag/*Shi Chang*/*puvacha*

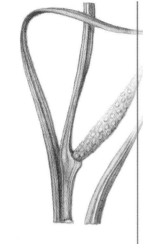

PARTS USED *rhizome* TASTE *pungent, bitter, astringent*
CHARACTER *warm* MERIDIANS *heart, stomach, liver*
ACTIONS *stimulant, rejuvenative tonic, antispasmodic,
decongestant, diaphoretic, emetic*

USES Sweet flag is used in all herbal traditions as a
cleansing stimulant and digestive remedy. In the West it
is mainly considered an appetite stimulant and a
remedy for stomach upsets. In China it clears "wind-
phlegm" and "dampness," which may be linked to
depression and poor digestion. In ayurveda it is used
for respiratory problems, including *vata* and *kapha* sore
throats, nervous upsets, shock, and digestive problems,
and is thought to improve memory and mental awareness.
CAUTIONS Do not use continuously for more than one
month; use is restricted in some countries; avoid in
excessive perspiration or bleeding disorders.

TERMINALIA SPP.   Myrobalan/*He Zi*/*bibhitaki*

PARTS USED *fruit* TASTE *astringent, sour/sweet/bitter*
CHARACTER *warm* MERIDIANS *lung, large intestine*
ACTIONS *astringent, rejuvenative tonic, expectorant,
laxative, anthelmintic, antiseptic*

USES *Bibhitaki (T. belerica)* is used in ayurveda mainly
as a *kapha* tonic, helping to strengthen the lungs,
voice, and vision. It is used for sore throats and
laryngitis, coughs, and catarrh. The unripe fruit is a
good laxative and is also used to expel intestinal
parasites. The ripe fruit is preferred for indigestion and
diarrhea. *Bibhitaki* is often combined with *haritaki/
He Zi (T. chebula)* in *triphala*, a classic laxative and
antiseptic tonic for the digestive system. *He Zi* is used
in China for diarrhea, coughs, and a hoarse voice.
CAUTIONS Avoid all *Terminalia* spp. in pregnancy and
severe exhaustion or excess heat syndromes.

OTHER HERBS THAT MAY BE HELPFUL
elder (p.55) ● *echinacea (p.45)* ● *He Shou Wu (p.179)*
● *Nu Zhen Zi (p.121)* ● *passion-flower (p.115)*

DRIED ECHINACEA

Ear problems

In the West most minor ailments affecting the ears are

regarded as being due either to catarrh or infection: typical

remedies include elder and echinacea. More serious conditions, such as

Ménière's disease with vertigo and nausea, are explained in terms of an

imbalance in the inner ear (labyrinth) where a delicate fluid mechanism

helps us to maintain our physical awareness. Deafness and tinnitus may

be linked to catarrhal problems, although more often they are dismissed

as being of unknown cause, with only limited treatment available.

In TCM the ear is closely linked to the kidney and to the vital essence

(Jing) stored there. Jing is believed to decline naturally with age, so

problems such as deafness and tinnitus, which are more common as we

grow older, are seen as a symptom of this inevitable decline. Kidney Qi

deficiency can also involve hearing problems at any age, so deafness is

regarded as a significant symptom in diagnosis. Ear problems are likely to

be treated with tonic herbs such as fleeceflower (p.179).

In ayurveda ear pains are generally treated with ghee

or medicated oils. Inflammations—a fire problem—are

treated with oils containing anti-pitta herbs; mucous

DROPPER

discharges are regarded as kapha and are treated with

more drying herbs. Vertigo is linked to wind or air and

is treated with anti-vata herbs. Tinnitus, too, is

a vata disorder; one treatment is to rub

castor oil on the soles of the feet.

REHMANNIA GLUTINOSA   Chinese foxglove/*Shu Di Huang*

PARTS USED *tuberous root* TASTE *sweet* CHARACTER *slightly warm* MERIDIANS *heart, liver, kidney* ACTIONS *cardiotonic, diuretic, mild laxative, hypoglycemic*

USES *Shu Di Huang* is the prepared form of the herb, made by stir-frying the sliced tubers with wine. It is a nourishing blood tonic and helps kidney *Yin* and *Jing*. It is used in blood disorders such as anemia, irregular menstruation, and abnormal uterine bleeding and also combats typical kidney-deficiency symptoms of low back pain, deafness, and night sweats. The raw herb, *Sheng Di Huang*, is colder and is sometimes cooked (without wine) to produce *Gan Di Huang*. Both of these forms are more helpful for *Yin* and body fluids, as well as being used to clear heat.

CAUTIONS Avoid in diarrhea and indigestion.

VERBASCUM THAPSUS   Mullein

PARTS USED *flowers, aerial parts* TASTE *slightly sweet* CHARACTER *cool, moist* MERIDIANS *lung, stomach, urinary bladder* ACTIONS *expectorant, demulcent, mild diuretic, sedative, wound healer, astringent, anti-inflammatory*

USES Mullein is a tall biennial with yellow flowers and leaves covered in thick, woolly down. The flowers were once the preferred part and were used in cough syrups and infused oils. They make a good, relaxing expectorant for all sorts of dry, chronic, hard coughs (such as in whooping cough, tuberculosis, asthma, and bronchitis) and are soothing for throat inflammations, including tracheitis, laryngitis, and tonsillitis. Mullein flowers also relieve hay-fever symptoms. The infused oil is used to soothe inflammations and wounds—including sores, boils, chilblains, and piles—while drops may be used to ease earache.

CAUTIONS None noted.

53

OTHER HERBS THAT MAY BE HELPFUL
myrrh (p.49) ● peppermint (p.79) ● yarrow (p.133) ● eyebright (p.65)
● camphor (p.157) ● betony (p.121) ● garlic (p.128)
● eucalyptus (p.197) ● marshmallow (p.78) ● camomile (p.192)

DRIED PEPPERMINT

Sinusitis and catarrh

Orthodox Western medicine links nasal catarrh with inflamed mucous membranes in the respiratory tract, which is usually caused by either an infection or an allergic response. Herbalists take a rather more holistic view, linking excess mucus with dietary imbalance—usually too many unrefined sugars or dairy products—as well as with lifestyle factors, such as working in stuffy environments and having too little fresh air and outdoor exercise.

They also classify the catarrh as "hot" (thick, yellow, and likely to be infected) or "cold" (clear, watery, and more related to damp problems).

> **SINUSES**
>
> The sinuses are cavities in the skull, around the eyes and nose, that reduce the bone weight. They are lined with mucous membranes and may become inflamed (sinusitis) or blocked by fluid or pus during a cold.

These different types of catarrh are treated with cooling or warming herbs respectively, to restore balance. There is an emotional dimension as well, with persistent sinus problems often being linked to blocked tears or an inability to "let go" and cry.

Chinese and ayurvedic theory similarly classify catarrh into "cold" and "hot." In TCM it is related especially to "wind" and is an aspect of "wind-heat" or "wind-cold syndromes," leading to blockage in the nasal passages. In ayurveda diet is also important, with hot, pitta-type congestion (rather like Western herbalism's "hot" variety) treated with more cooling, damp, or kapha-promoting herbs and foods, while the opposite approach is needed for kapha or cold/damp types of catarrh.

SAMBUCUS NIGRA Elder

PARTS USED *flowers* TASTE *bitter, slightly sweet*
CHARACTER *cool, dry* MERIDIANS *lung, bladder*
ACTIONS *expectorant, anticatarrhal, circulatory stimulant, diaphoretic, diuretic, anti-inflammatory*

USES The elder tree was once regarded as a complete medicine chest, since all parts could be used in some way. The berries are a source of vitamin C, so they acted as a prophylactic for winter colds, as well as being diuretic and laxative. The bark and root made strong purgatives, while the leaves were the basis of "green ointment," a household wound healer. Today only the flowers are widely used; they seem to strengthen the mucous membranes of the upper respiratory tract so, although some argue that the herb can cause hay fever, may increase resistance to irritant allergens.
CAUTIONS None noted for the flowers.

XANTHIUM SIBIRICUM *Cang Er Zi*

PARTS USED *fruit* TASTE *pungent, bitter* CHARACTER *warm, slightly toxic* MERIDIANS *lung* ACTIONS *antibacterial, antifungal, antirheumatic, antispasmodic, analgesic*

USES Traditionally *Cang Er Zi* is used in TCM to "open the aperture of the nose" and dispel wind and damp—which are seen as a cause of both common colds and rheumatic/arthritic problems known as "*Bi* syndrome." It is used for allergic rhinitis, chronic catarrh, and sinus problems, and is combined with mint, a type of angelica, and magnolia flowers in *Cang Er San*, a popular powdered formula used for sinusitis. It will also ease pain and skin itching and was traditionally used for leprosy and other skin conditions.
CAUTIONS Contains a compound called xanthistrumarin, which can affect blood-sugar levels, so avoid in diabetes.

OTHER HERBS THAT MAY BE HELPFUL

sage (p.49) ● echinacea (p.45) ● garlic (p.128) ● thyme (p.43)
● myrrh (p.49) ● guggul (p.119) ● eucalyptus (p.197)
● yarrow (p.133) ● raspberry (p.185) ● slippery elm (p.93).

Tonsils, mumps, and swollen glands

What are popularly termed "swollen glands" are more

often than not enlarged lymph nodes. The lymphatic system

is part of the network for conveying various fluids around

the body, while the nodes play a part in the immune system.

Glandular fever involves swellings in these nodes as a result of viral

infection. Tonsils are patches of lymphatic tissue in the throat, so swelling

and inflammation here can also suggest some sort of infection. Mumps

(parotitis) is also seen as an infection—inflammation of the parotid glands,

one of the three pairs of glands that produce saliva.

Western herbalists use a combination of anti-inflammatory and antiviral

herbs with lymphatic cleansers to treat these sorts of problems.

Lacking the necessary anatomical knowledge (since they did not dissect

bodies or know the difference between different sorts of glands), the

Chinese took a simpler approach, classifying these sorts of "lumps and

hard swellings" together. If the swellings are hot and inflamed, then "fire

poisons"—heat and toxins—are blamed. Cooling herbs, often also anti-

microbial, are used to disperse them. Cooler swellings may be seen as a

fluid or water problem and are treated with diuretics.

Ayurveda makes a similar distinction, with

humoral imbalance being seen as the cause: hot

problems suggest excess pitta; *colder swellings a*

surfeit of kapha.

FORSYTHIA SUSPENSA *Lian Qiao*

PARTS USED *fruit* TASTE *bitter* CHARACTER *slightly cold*
MERIDIANS *lung, heart, gall bladder* ACTIONS *antibacterial, anti-emetic, antiparasitic*

USES Forsythia is familiar in the West as a garden shrub, brought to Europe in 1844 and named after the botanist William Forsyth (1737–1804), who was head gardener at Kensington Palace. The herb is mainly used in China to clear heat and fire poisons, expel wind-heat, and dissipate nodules and swellings. It is an effective herb for clearing any infection or abscess and is traditionally used for feverish colds, characterized by sore throats and headaches. It is also effective for infections involving swollen neck glands or lymph nodes and for urinary-tract infections.

CAUTIONS Avoid in diarrhea with "deficient spleen," fevers linked to "deficient *Qi*" and purulent abscesses.

GALIUM APARINE **Bedstraw**

PARTS USED *aerial parts* TASTE *bitter, salty* CHARACTER *cold, dry* MERIDIANS *liver, bladder* ACTIONS *diuretic, lymphatic cleanser, mild astringent*

USES Generally dismissed as a weed, bedstraw (also known as sticky willy or sweetheart) can be found in most suburban gardens. It is an important lymphatic cleanser once used to feed geese—hence its country name, "goosegrass." It was a traditional ingredient in "spring tonics" used to cleanse and restore the system after the dietary deficiencies of winter. It is best used fresh, pulped in a food processor and taken as a diuretic and lymphatic cleanser, and is effective for enlarged lymph nodes. It is also used when the body is failing to rid itself of toxins, including skin problems and rheumatism. The cream is effective for psoriasis.

CAUTIONS None noted.

Holistic health tips

• Dairy products and refined carbohydrates encourage mucus production (in ayurveda they are defined as kapha-forming), so avoid both when suffering from nasal catarrh, colds, or coughs.

• Steam inhalants can help to clear a stuffy nose as well as relieve allergic conditions. Try thyme or hyssop for chesty colds or camomile flowers for mild asthma attacks or hay fever. Use 1oz/25g of dried herb to 2½pt/1.25 litres boiling water. Leave to infuse thoroughly for 4–5 minutes, then inhale the steam for 10–15 minutes. Stay in a warm room for at least 30 minutes after treatment.

• Chest rubs can help to relieve congestion in coughs and colds. Add 5 drops of essential oil of hyssop, eucalyptus, thyme, or tea tree to 1tsp/5ml of almond oil and massage gently into the front and back of the chest.

• In traditional gem therapy blue stones, such as aquamarine and lapis lazuli, are associated with the voice, communications, and the throat chakra. For habitual throat problems or to increase confidence in public speaking, wear an aquamarine necklace or ring.

• Members of the onion family all have similar antibacterial and anticatarrhal properties to garlic and can be used in simple therapeutic remedies at home for coughs, nasal catarrh, and congestion. Eat plenty of French onion soup and steamed or sautéed leeks. Make a simple syrup by layering slices of onion with honey or brown sugar; leave overnight to let the onion juice mix with the sugar, then strain and take in 1tsp/5ml doses for coughs or chest infections.

• A 24-hour fruit fast—eating only fresh fruit throughout the day—can be helpful for combating colds and catarrhal conditions.

EYES, SKIN, AND HAIR
Western Approach

Above *Minor eye problems may be self-limiting, but can indicate underlying problems.*

Below *Rose was traditionally said to be good for both "the skin and the soul."*

Orthodox medicine tends to regard many minor or self-limiting inflammations affecting the skin and eyes as being due to infection and treats them with antibiotics and anti-inflammatories. Chronic skin conditions, such as severe eczema, are often simply treated with stronger anti-inflammatory drugs (usually steroids) in an approach that will efficiently suppress the symptoms, but which does little to solve the underlying problem.

Western herbalists take a more holistic view, looking at diet, possible allergies, emotional states, and lifestyle, and not just the physical symptoms. Recurrent eye problems are often indicative of exhaustion and stress, while food intolerance may be a factor in some skin disorders. Allergic reactions are certainly increasing and are not being helped by high levels of pesticides, growth hormones, and antibiotics in the food that we eat. All these pollutants can strain the liver as it attempts to filter these substances and prevent them reentering the bloodstream. Many herbalists routinely include cleansing liver remedies, such as dandelion, in prescriptions for the skin.

Various skin problems also have a psychological dimension: an unsightly skin rash, for example, may be a physical manifestation of an insecure or introverted individual, sending out a "keep away, don't touch me" message. In such cases, relaxing nervines to ease inner tensions, plus gentle help from Bach Flower Remedies or remedies such as rose, which affect the emotions and spirit, can work wonders.

EYES, SKIN, AND HAIR
Chinese Approach

TCM connects the eyes, skin, and hair with the major *Zang* (solid) organs of the body within the framework of the five-element model. The eyes are linked to the liver, the skin to the lungs, and head hair to the kidney. Body hair is considered to be separate from head hair and is also associated with the lungs.

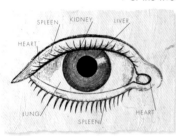

Above *The eye is a useful mirror for the five* Zang *organs, with different parts of the eye indicating each solid organ.*

Weaknesses in the energy levels of any of these *Zang* organs, or an imbalance of *Yin* and *Yang*, is seen outwardly in disorders of the eyes, skin, or hair. Poor eyesight, tired eyes, or inflammation of the eye is an indication that the liver is out of order. Chinese tradition maintains that the alertness which can be seen in the eyes of someone who is fully conscious of their surroundings is an indication of *Shen*, or spirit.

Traditional theory maintains that the vital essence (*Jing*) stored in the kidney is transformed into bone marrow, which spreads along the spinal cord to the brain. Through this connection with the bones and brain the kidney is thus associated with head hair—an abundance of lustrous hair is believed to indicate healthy kidney *Qi*, and thus creativity. Children born with plenty of hair that does not fall out in the first weeks are expected to be vigorous, creative individuals. Graying or falling hair suggests kidney weakness.

Below *Graying hair is treated with kidney tonics in TCM.*

Skin is not only linked to the lungs, but also to *Wei Qi* or defense energy: this travels on the surface, so healthy skin suggests strong immunity. To a good practitioner, skin color indicates inner balance and harmony: pallor suggests *Yang* deficiency, while an over-red skin may imply inner heat or excess *Yang*.

EYES, SKIN, AND HAIR
Ayurvedic Approach

Ayurveda usually analyses health problems in terms of humoral imbalance. Inflammations with red, irritated skin or eyes, for example, are associated with an excess of *pitta* (fire), while swellings or edema and oozing sores suggest a *kapha* problem.

Depending on individual humoral balance, these sorts of ailments may be more or less likely to occur. *Pitta* types, for example, are more likely to suffer from skin problems as their high heat levels are easily tipped into "critical" mode by excess *pitta*.

Pitta is also closely linked to the eyes as an organ of perception, so again *pitta* types are more likely to suffer from eye disorders and they will probably be more light-sensitive, needing sunglasses and possibly also suffering from a range of visual defects that require them to wear spectacles.

Above *Pitta types are often very sensitive to light and need to wear sunglasses.*

Below *Gemstones are used in ayurvedic eye treatments —pearls and silver for pitta-vata conditions; rubies and gold for kapha-vata ones.*

Crying is believed to be a good way of cleansing the eyes and ayurveda practitioners may suggest peeling onions regularly or applying a little dilute onion juice to the eye in order to start the tears flowing and to wash away any toxins. Some practitioners say that crying is a good way of cleansing the liver and blood. Gem therapy is also used in ayurveda eye treatments: wearing pearls to ease dry, inflamed eyes, for instance, or rubies in order to improve the eyesight.

OTHER HERBS THAT MAY BE HELPFUL
Dang Gui (p.173) ● *Bai Shao Yao (p.86)* ● *elder (p.55)*
● *camomile (p.192)*

PEONY

Eye problems

An orthodox Western approach to

eye problems usually focuses on

infection as the cause of many minor ailments.

Conjunctivitis (an inflammation affecting the white part of the eye,

also known as pink eye), blepharitis (affecting the eyelid), and styes (an

acute inflammation of a gland at the base of an eyelash) are all usually

blamed on bacterial infection. A more holistic approach links them to

lowered resistance and immune deficiency associated with stress,

overwork, or repeated infections. Western herbalists use antibacterial

remedies to treat the immediate problem and follow through with tonic

herbs to rebuild the weakened system.

In Chinese medicine the eye is closely linked to the liver. Poor eyesight is

seen as a result of "deficient liver blood," while irritant conditions such as

conjunctivitis are defined in terms of heat or wind affecting the liver or its

meridians, so remedies usually include herbs to normalize and calm the liver.

In ayurveda eye inflammations are associated with excess pitta and are usually treated with herbs that are traditionally regarded as cooling and calming but are now known to be effective antibacterials. Deteriorating eyesight in old age is linked to excess vata.

GHEE TREATMENT
A traditional ayurvedic remedy is to stare at the flame of a ghee lamp for 20 minutes a day to help strengthen the eyesight. Ghee (clarified butter) is believed to be generally helpful for eye problems, and two to three teaspoons are taken daily.

ALOE SPP. Aloe vera/*Lu Hui/kumari*

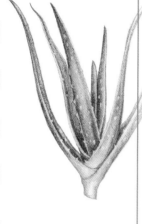

PARTS USED *sap, leaves* TASTE *astringent, sweet, bitter*
CHARACTER *cold, moist* MERIDIANS *liver, stomach, large
intestine* ACTIONS *purgative, stimulates bile flow, wound
healer, tonic, demulcent, antifungal, styptic, sedative, anthelmintic*

USES While the whole leaves of "bitter aloes" are a
purgative, the leaf sap or gel, known as aloe vera, is
used externally as a wound healer, to relieve burns and
skin problems (including eczema and thrush) and to
ease eye problems. In ayurveda it is used to reduce
excess *pitta* and is often taken with a pinch of turmeric
as a general tonic. The Chinese use it in order to
clear heat from the liver and large intestine and as a
digestive remedy.

CAUTIONS Avoid internally in pregnancy as aloe vera is
strongly purgative; high doses of the leaf extracts may
cause vomiting.

CALENDULA OFFICINALIS Marigold

PARTS USED *flowers, essential oil* TASTE *slightly bitter, pungent*
CHARACTER *drying, gently cooling* MERIDIANS *liver, heart*
ACTIONS *astringent, antiseptic, antifungal, anti-inflammatory,
antispasmodic, wound healer, menstrual regulator, immune
stimulant, diaphoretic, estrogenic*

USES Marigold is familiar in patent calendula creams
used for dry skin and eczema, but it is also a powerful
menstrual regulator, helpful for many gynecological
conditions, and a bitter digestive remedy. As an antifungal it is helpful for vaginal thrush and athlete's foot; it
is also detoxifying and is used in chronic infections.
Marigold can be used externally for a wide range of
skin problems and inflammations and is effective in
eyebaths for inflammations and styes. It is also valuable
internally for feverish or toxic conditions and to move
liver energies.

CAUTIONS None noted.

DENDRANTHEMA X GRANDIFLORUM · Chrysanthemum/*Ju Hua*

PARTS USED *flowers* TASTE *pungent, sweet, bitter*
CHARACTER *cool* MERIDIANS *lung, liver* ACTIONS *antibacterial, antifungal, antiviral, anti-inflammatory, hypotensive, peripheral vasodilator*

USES *Ju Hua* is used in China to disperse wind and heat and neutralize toxins; it is a specific to clear liver heat and calm liver wind. "Ascending liver *Yang*" and "wind-heat in the liver channel" are both associated with sore, red eyes, dizziness, and headaches. *Ju Hua* is good in both conditions, being said to "brighten the eyes" and being used for colds or feverish conditions where bloodshot eyes are a key characteristic. It also reduces high blood pressure.
CAUTIONS Avoid in diarrhea and *Qi* deficiency.

EMBLICA OFFICINALIS · Emblic myrobalan/*amalaki*

PARTS USED *fruit* TASTE *mainly salty, sweet and sour*
CHARACTER *cooling* MERIDIANS *liver, spleen, kidney*
ACTIONS *nutritive tonic, rejuvenative, aphrodisiac, laxative, astringent, stops bleeding*

USES *Amalaki* is also known as *dhatri*—both words meaning "the nurse"—due to its potent healing properties. It is a nutritive remedy and a *rasayana* (longevity tonic, *see p. 106*) for *pitta* conditions. It is used for all bleeding disorders and is said to cleanse the mouth, strengthen the teeth, and nourish the bones. It is also traditionally believed to improve the eyesight and is a major ingredient in *chyavan prash*—a herbal jelly used in India as a general tonic and to strengthen the eyes. *Amalaki* also eases digestive problems, normalizes blood-sugar levels, and helps increase red-blood cell levels, so it is ideal in anemia. The fruits are a very rich source of vitamin C (up to 3g per fruit).
CAUTIONS Avoid in diarrhea or dysentery.

EUPHRASIA OFFICINALIS Eyebright

PARTS USED *aerial parts* TASTE *astringent, pungent* CHARACTER *cool, dry* MERIDIANS *lung, spleen, large intestine* ACTIONS *anti-inflammatory, antihistaminic, anticatarrhal, astringent*

USES A tiny, semi-parasitic plant growing in grassy meadows, eyebright—as its common name suggests—has been used as a remedy for eye problems since at least the fourteenth century. It is used in eyebaths for conjunctivitis and other inflammations and can also be taken internally (often in tablets and capsules) to relieve the more irritant symptoms of hay fever or allergic rhinitis. It is also an effective anticatarrhal for sinusitis and catarrh.

CAUTIONS None noted.

FOENICULUM VULGARE Fennel/*Xiao Hui Xiang*/*shatapushpa*

PARTS USED *seeds* TASTE *pungent* CHARACTER *warm* MERIDIANS *stomach, liver, kidney* ACTIONS *anti-inflammatory, carminative, circulatory stimulant, galactogogue, mild expectorant, diuretic*

USES Fennel seeds have been mainly regarded in the West as a digestive remedy to ease colic, chills, and indigestion and to stimulate milk flow in nursing mothers. The seeds are also good for easing tired and sore eyes, used either in infusions or with soaked teabags applied as eyepads. In China fennel seeds are believed to help regulate *Qi*, alleviate pain, and warm both stomach and middle *Jiao*. The seeds are also used as a digestive remedy in ayurveda and are believed both to calm the nerves and encourage mental alertness.

CAUTIONS Use cautiously in "deficient *Yin*" and avoid high doses in pregnancy.

OTHER HERBS THAT MAY BE HELPFUL
dandelion (p.87) ● *red clover (p.179)* ● *isphagula (p.89)*
● *yarrow (p.133)* ● *turmeric (p.130)* ● *sandalwood (p.81)*
● *guggul (p.119)* ● *Jin Yin Hua (p.45)* ● *Lian Qiao (p.57)*

ALOE VERA

Skin

Western herbalists associate skin problems with infections, poor

circulation, hormonal imbalance, allergies, diet, and stress. Conditions

such as teenage acne may be due to a combination of some of these, so

treatment needs to cover the relevant aspects. Similarly, some types of

eczema can be associated with a food allergy and are exacerbated by

stress, so treatment may include dietary advice and calming nervines.

Other skin irritations may be the result of poor circulation and inadequate

excretion, leading to a build-up of toxins, so cleansing herbs (known as

depuratives) may be chosen.

In Chinese theory skin problems have a similarly mixed origin. Some

are associated with "external evils"—notably heat and wind—leading to

red, dry, irritant rashes. Others are blamed on excess heat in the blood,

so blood-cooling herbs, such as Chi Shao Yao, are chosen. Exact diagnosis

is important. Skin is associated with the lungs, with healthy, glowing skin

indicating strong lung Qi. It is also associated with resistance to "external

evils," since the defense energy Wei Qi resides on the surface.

In ayurveda humoral imbalance is seen as a cause of skin

problems. Irritant, red rashes associated

with infection, irritability, and fever are

linked to excess pitta; dry, scaly skin

problems with itching and possibly

digestive weakness, to vata; oozing sores

with swelling and itchiness, to kapha.

PLANTAIN LEAVES

ARCTIUM LAPPA Burdock/*Niu Bang*

PARTS USED *leaves, root, seeds* **TASTE** *pungent, bitter*
CHARACTER *cold* **MERIDIANS**: *lung, stomach* **ACTIONS**
*leaves—mild laxative, diuretic; root—cleansing, mild laxative,
diuretic, diaphoretic, antirheumatic, antiseptic, antibiotic; seeds
—febrifugal, anti-inflammatory, antibacterial, hypoglycemic*

USES Burdock root has long been used as a cleansing
herb for chronic skin and rheumatic problems and
wherever a sluggish digestion is contributing to a build-
up of toxins. Traditionally it was combined with
dandelion as a popular cleansing cordial. The leaf is
less effective than the root, but is still used for stomach
problems such as indigestion and weakness. In China
the seeds, known as *Niu Bang Zi*, are used for treating
feverish colds, measles, acute tonsillitis, and abscesses,
while modern research suggests antimicrobial activity.
CAUTIONS Avoid *Niu Bang Zi* in diarrhea.

AZADIRACHTA INDICA Neem/*nimba*

PARTS USED *bark, seeds, leaves, resin* **TASTE** *bitter, pungent*
CHARACTER *cooling* **MERIDIANS** *spleen, lung* **ACTIONS** *anti-
inflammatory, antifungal, bitter tonic, expels worms, prevents
vomiting, cleansing, reduces fevers*

USES Neem is believed to encourage the *vata* humor,
while reducing *pitta* and *kapha*, so it is taken for
obesity and diabetes. The bark has been used for
malaria, tuberculosis, diabetes, tumors, arthritis, and
rheumatic problems, while the resin is used in soaps
and toothpastes. The seed oil is traditionally used as a
contraceptive. It is also used in commercial hair lotions
and is strongly antibacterial. The crushed seeds are
made into a paste for treating piles. The juice, made
by crushing the fresh leaves, is used in ointments for
eczema and ringworm.
CAUTIONS Do not give to the elderly, very young, or weak.

OENOTHERA BIENNIS Evening-primrose

PARTS USED *seed oil* TASTE *astringent, bitter*
CHARACTER *warming* MERIDIANS *spleen, lung*
ACTIONS *anti-eczema, demulcent, antithrombotic*

....

USES Evening-primrose is rich in an essential fatty acid called gamma-linolenic acid (GLA), a precursor of prostaglandin E_1—a hormone-like chemical that inhibits abnormal cell proliferation. GLA is normally metabolized in the body from other naturally occurring acids, but the process can be affected by poor diet and high cholesterol levels. Lack of GLA has been associated with systemic rheumatic and skin disorders, including severe eczema. The oil is reputed to ease menstrual and menopausal problems (including irritable bowel syndrome), strengthen the circulatory system, and boost the immune system.

CAUTIONS None noted.

PAEONIA LACTIFLORA Red peony/*Chi Shao Yao*

PARTS USED *root* TASTE *sour, bitter* CHARACTER *slightly cold* MERIDIANS *liver, spleen* ACTIONS *antibacterial, anti-inflammatory, anticoagulant, immune stimulant, reduces cholesterol levels, peripheral vasodilator, hypoglycemic, sedative, stimulates tissue repair, improves microcirculation*

....

USES Red peony (the color relates to the root, not the flower) has been used in China since AD 500. It is one of the main blood stimulants, helping circulation and clearing stagnation. It also affects the liver meridian and clears "liver fire," so is used for menstrual disorders. It is a cooling remedy and specific for "hot blood" syndromes, which can include irritant skin disorders; it is sometimes used for clearing abscesses and boils. It was used in trials at London's Great Ormond Street Hospital for children suffering from severe eczema.

CAUTIONS Avoid if there is no sign of blood stagnation.

PHELLODENDRON CHINENSE   Chinese corktree/*Huang Bai*

PARTS USED *bark* TASTE *bitter* CHARACTER *cold*
MERIDIANS *kidney, urinary bladder, large intestine*
ACTIONS *antibacterial, hypoglycemic, bile stimulant, diuretic, peripheral vasodilator, febrifugal, sedative*

USES *Huang Bai* means "yellow fir" and, along with *Huang Lian (Coptis chinensis)* and *Huang Qin (p.137)*, it is one of the three important Chinese "yellow" herbs used to clear heat and dampness from the system. It is used for diarrhea, jaundice, and acute urinary-tract infections, as well as for treating abscesses, eczema, boils, and other "damp" skin lesions that are associated with heat and "fire poisons." It also combats heat symptoms associated with *Jing* or *Yin* deficiency and "ascending kidney fire."
CAUTIONS Avoid in "deficient spleen" and in diarrhea associated with cold or weak stomach.

STELLARIA MEDIA   Chickweed

PARTS USED *aerial parts* TASTE *sweet, salty* CHARACTER *cold, moist* MERIDIANS *stomach, heart, lung, large intestine*
ACTIONS *astringent, antirheumatic, wound healer, demulcent*

USES As its name implies, chickweed has long been used for feeding domestic fowl. It is an extremely common garden weed and makes a popular, soothing cream for irritant skin rashes and eczema. It can also be used in the first-aid kit for burns, boils, and for drawing splinters. It was once regarded as a significant source of vitamin C, with sprigs of chickweed being added to salads or cooked as a vegetable.
CAUTIONS None noted.

OTHER HERBS THAT MAY BE HELPFUL
gotu kola (p.106) ● amalaki (p.64), ● licorice (p.41)
● sandalwood (p.81) ● He Shou Wu (p.179) ● Gou Qi Zi (p.85)
● Shu Di Huang (p.53) ● Nu Zhen Zi (p.121)

ALMONDS

Hair problems

**In orthodox medicine hair problems are often dismissed
as being merely cosmetic, but to herbalists they can signify
underlying imbalance and weaknesses. In Chinese medicine head hair is
associated with the kidney, so falling or prematurely graying hair may
indicate kidney Qi weakness, as well as being the natural consequence
of the run-down of Jing (vital essence) in old age. Ayurveda connects
premature hair loss with excess pitta and recommends an anti-pitta diet
that is high in dairy products, almonds, and sesame seeds—all of which
promote hair growth. Sudden alopecia (baldness) is more likely to be
related to a vata problem.**

ECLIPTA PROSTATA   *Han Lian Cao/bhringaraj*

PARTS USED *aerial parts* TASTE *sweet, sour* CHARACTER *cold*
MERIDIANS *liver, kidney* ACTIONS *astringent, antibacterial,
tonic, alterative, styptic, febrifugal, nervine, laxative, wound
healer*

USES *Bhringaraj* is important in both ayurvedic and
Chinese medicine as a kidney tonic, especially if there
is tinnitus or premature graying hair. Its Indian name
actually means "ruler of the hair" and, as in Chinese
theory, healthy head hair is said to indicate healthy
kidneys. It is a *Yin* tonic, nourishes the liver, and stops
bleeding, so it is also taken for heavy menstrual or
postpartum bleeding. It combats aging and helps
rejuvenate bones, teeth, sight, hearing, and memory. It
also calms the mind and encourages restful sleep.
CAUTIONS Avoid in cold and "deficient spleen and
kidney," or in severe chills.

ROSMARINUS OFFICINALIS   Rosemary

PARTS USED *leaves, essential oil* TASTE *pungent, bitter* CHARACTER *warming, dry* MERIDIANS *lung, spleen, heart, liver* ACTIONS *astringent, digestive remedy, nervine, carminative, antiseptic, diuretic, diaphoretic, antidepressive, circulatory stimulant, antispasmodic, restorative tonic for the nervous system, bile stimulant, cardiac tonic*

USES Rosemary is a stimulating tonic herb—very warming and useful for temporary fatigue and overwork. It makes a pleasant tea. The herb will also stimulate the circulation and can relieve headaches, migraines, indigestion, and the cold feelings that come with poor circulation. The oil is a valuable remedy for arthritis, rheumatism, and muscular aches and pains. Rosemary is reputed to darken graying hair, but it also makes a good rinse for auburn hair and will help to clear dandruff.

CAUTIONS None noted.

URTICA DIOICA   Stinging nettle

PARTS USED *aerial parts, root* TASTE *astringent, slightly bitter* CHARACTER *cool, dry* MERIDIANS *liver, spleen, urinary bladder* ACTIONS *astringent, diuretic, tonic, nutritive, hemostatic, circulatory stimulant, promotes milk production, hypoglycemic, antiscorbutic*

USES Nettles sting because the hairs on their stems and leaves contain histamine, a potent irritant for the skin. They make an ideal "spring tonic" to cleanse the system and are helpful in chronic skin conditions and arthritis. Their high mineral content may be helpful for dry or falling hair, while extracts of nettle leaf are added to shampoos and rinses. Externally, nettle oil and ointments can be used for skin problems and rheumatic pain. The root is a central European remedy to strengthen the hair and may ease prostate problems.

CAUTIONS None noted.

Holistic health tips

• *Many ready-made herbal teabags make ideal eye-pads for tired or strained eyes after they have been used to produce tea: infuse fennel or camomile teabags in the usual way and drink the tea, and then place the cooled bags over your closed eyes and relax for 10–15 minutes.*

• *Emerald ash (panna bhasma) is used in ayurvedic gem therapy to treat skin diseases as well as infections and ulcers. Emerald is cooling and energizing—for irritant skin inflammations. Peridot or jade makes a more economical substitute—wear a ring set in silver on the middle finger.*

• *Repeated eye infections, such as styes and conjunctivitis, usually suggest a weakened immune system, probably due to stress or overwork. Combine any specific remedies with rest, relaxation, and herbs like Huang Qi to strengthen the defenses.*

• *Crushed pearls are traditionally swallowed with water as a powder in China, and are given to small children to ensure a beautiful skin. Wear pearls next to the skin for a rather more economical alternative.*

• *Combat premature graying hair with rinses of rosemary and stinging nettles, as well as kidney tonics like Nu Zhen Zi and He Shou Wu.*

DIGESTIVE SYSTEM
Western Approach

Above *Mint is helpful for many types of digestive disorder. The leaves of the plant are used.*

Below *Eating "on the run" and having a poorly balanced diet can lead to indigestion and more serious health problems.*

Medieval Western herbalists used to say that "death dwells in the bowels," reflecting the importance of an efficient digestive function in maintaining health. Herbal medicine contains an enormous repertoire of digestive remedies aimed at soothing or stimulating, relaxing or regulating this function.

Unlike modern orthodox remedies, which often seem to offer little more than antacids or laxatives, herbal remedies include carminatives to clear wind; liver and pancreatic stimulants to encourage normal function; antispasmodics to relieve cramps; and anti-microbials to normalize gut flora and increase resistance to invading bacteria—notably *Helicobacter pylori*, which is now believed to be the bacteria responsible for gastric ulceration.

Modern medicine tends to analyse our digestive function purely in physiological terms, with enzymes breaking down the nutrients from our food, followed by absorption mechanisms and efficient excretion from the body, with the liver being relegated to the role of chemical factory, processing fats and breakdown products.

While traditional Galenic medicine also focuses on function and efficiency, it adds into the equation the intrinsic character of the foods we eat, warning, for example, that cold foods eaten in winter will increase the risk of stomach chills, while roasted meats eaten in summer will increase inner heat levels and thus lead to imbalance.

73

DIGESTIVE SYSTEM
Chinese Approach

Above *Black pepper stimulates and warms the digestive tract and is reputed to clear toxins from the system.*

In Chinese theory the organs primarily associated with digestive function are the spleen and stomach. The concept of "spleen" is, however, very different from that of Western anatomy. To the Chinese the spleen is central to digestion and muscle development; it is traditionally believed to absorb the various nutrients from food and then to stimulate the dispersal of this "food essence" through the body. If spleen *Qi* is strong, digestion works well and the body is healthy; if it is weak, then tissues become malnourished. The spleen performs the same function with water extracted from food, sending it through the body to reach the kidneys.

The stomach is the corresponding *Fu* (hollow) organ to the spleen *(see p. 16)*. Its role is to take in and digest food and it is regarded as the reservoir for food and water supplies. Its effectiveness in starting the digestive process is seen as a function of stomach *Qi* —if this is strong, then the food is propelled onward to the small intestine; if it is weak, then food tends to stagnate in the stomach. Spleen and stomach are very closely associated and the two terms are sometimes used interchangeably.

Chinese medicine incorporates another digestive concept, known as the "triple burner" or *San Jiao*, sometimes described as a formless sewage system. It is perhaps best regarded as a generalization of internal functions related to water regulation and digestion. It has three components—upper, middle, and lower *Jiao*—with the middle *Jiao* being closely linked to the functions of the spleen and stomach.

Above *The spleen is believed to be responsible for building strong limbs and well-developed muscles.*

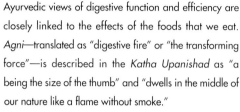

DIGESTIVE SYSTEM
Ayurvedic Approach

Ayurvedic views of digestive function and efficiency are closely linked to the effects of the foods that we eat. *Agni*—translated as "digestive fire" or "the transforming force"—is described in the *Katha Upanishad* as "a being the size of the thumb" and "dwells in the middle of our nature like a flame without smoke."

KAPHA

PITTA

VATA

This inner fire is responsible for processing foods, extracting nutrients, destroying invading pathogens, and clearing wastes. Abnormalities in *agni* are likely to be seen as poor digestive function, poor circulation, poor complexion or skin quality, a weakened immune system, unpleasant body odors, constipation, and excessive flatulence.

Agni may be high, low, variable, or balanced. It tends to be high in *pitta*-types who have excessive appetite but burn off the nutrients efficiently. In *kapha*-types *agni* tends to be low and there is poor appetite and weight gain, even with minimal food intake. In *vata*-types *agni* is more variable, with alternating bouts of extreme hunger and poor appetite. The ideal is balanced *agni*, where there is a normal, regular appetite, easily satisfied hunger, and regular bowel movements.

Digestion is believed to occur in three stages. The first is *kapha* (damp), occurring in the mouth and stomach where water and earth elements are extracted from the food. Next is a *pitta* (bile) stage, with acids in the stomach and small intestine extracting the fire element. Finally in the *vata* (wind) phase, the air and ether elements are extracted in the large intestine.

Above *Digestion is divided into three stages, which are dominated by* kapha, pitta, *and* vata.

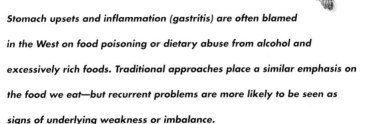

OTHER HERBS THAT MAY BE HELPFUL
meadowsweet (p.184) ● camomile (p.192) ● lemon-balm (p.111)
● ginger (p.185) ● turmeric (p.130) ● agrimony (p.192)
● catmint (p.198) ● rosemary (p.71)

Stomach upsets and appetite problems

DRIED CAMOMILE

Stomach upsets and inflammation (gastritis) are often blamed

in the West on food poisoning or dietary abuse from alcohol and

excessively rich foods. Traditional approaches place a similar emphasis on

the food we eat—but recurrent problems are more likely to be seen as

signs of underlying weakness or imbalance.

For modern Western herbalists, digestion is central to health: poor

digestive function is not only likely to lead to obvious upsets, constipation

or diarrhea, but is linked to systemic problems

such as skin disorders and arthritic ailments.

There is now increasing concern over food

intolerance in our polluted environment,

with symptoms ranging from abdominal bloating

to muscular pains and even neurological

disturbances. Food intolerance may sometimes trigger

a full-blown allergic response with irritant rashes and

swelling, as in cases of salicylate allergy. More often,

however, the reaction is "masked" as the body struggles

to overcome the stresses caused by a particular food.

ROSEMARY

As well as conditions like eczema and asthma, food intolerance may be

associated with digestive upsets, migraines, lethargy, and diarrhea.

Chinese medicine is more likely to define stomach upsets and

imbalances in terms of spleen Qi weakness. Deficiency here can lead to excess production of phlegm, as the spleen fails to separate the "turbid" products of digestion from the clear. Symptoms will depend on where the phlegm is concentrated. If it is in the stomach, then it will lead to nausea and vomiting; in the lung, to coughing and shortness of breath; in the heart, to mental disturbances, coma, or delirium; and so on.

"Deficient spleen or stomach Qi" or "spleen Yang deficiency" are common causes of excess phlegm, with symptoms such as poor appetite, abdominal bloating and discomfort, tiredness, and a tendency toward loose stools or diarrhea. It is the sort of problem that might be labelled "irritable bowel syndrome" in Western medicine and may be associated with nervous indigestion or a tendency toward gastric ulcers.

In ayurvedic medicine the stomach is associated with the first stage in digestion and is a kapha organ; the body's kapha levels and condition are said to be indicated by the state of the stomach. Kapha is sometimes described as the humor that "holds things together," so kapha problems may be linked to emotional upsets and worry, which thus manifest themselves as stomach upsets.

Disorders are generally defined in terms of their humoral imbalance and the effect they have on this kapha organ. Excess acidity and gastritis, for example, are pitta disorders, to be treated with an anti-pitta diet—one low in hot, spicy foods—as well as cooling herbs.

Suitable remedies to normalize agni are also important: hot spices if agni is low; cooling bitters if it is high; as well as harmonizing herbs to help maintain normal function where it is balanced.

FRUIT AND VEGETABLES

ALTHAEA OFFICINALIS Marshmallow

PARTS USED *root, leaves, flowers* TASTE *sweet*
CHARACTER *cool and moist* MERIDIANS *lung, stomach,
large intestine, urinary bladder* ACTIONS *root and
leaves—demulcent, expectorant, diuretic, wound healer;
flowers—expectorant*

USES Marshmallow can be used for bronchitis, irritating
coughs, and cystitis. The root is especially soothing for
the digestive system, helping to ease inflammation of
the mucous membranes in conditions such as heartburn,
gastritis, enteritis, esophagitis, and peptic ulceration,
and to ease the symptoms of hiatus hernia. It can be
used externally for wounds, burns, and boils and has a
soothing effect on the skin. The leaves are similar in
action to the root, but are slightly less demulcent. They
are used mainly for bronchial and urinary disorders
where soothing, healing properties are needed.

CAUTIONS None noted.

ATRACTYLODES MACROCEPHALA *Bai Zhu*

PARTS USED *rhizome* TASTE *sweet, bitter* CHARACTER *warm*
MERIDIANS *spleen, stomach* ACTIONS *antibacterial, anticoagulant, digestive stimulant, diuretic, hypoglycemic*

USES *Bai Zhu* is one of the main *Qi* tonics, used
especially for spleen or stomach *Qi* deficiency
syndromes, with typical symptoms likely to include
diarrhea, tiredness, abdominal bloating, poor appetite,
and nausea. It is also said to "dry dampness" and is
used for edema and fluid retention as well as to control
excess sweating and strengthen resistance. The herb is
included in a famous energy-giving remedy known as
"four noble ingredients decoction" *(Si Jun Zi Tang)*, with
Ren Shen (p. 106), *Fu Ling (p. 169)*, and *Gan Cao* or
licorice *(p. 41)*.

CAUTIONS Avoid in "deficient *Yin*" with extreme thirst.

DIOSCOREA SPP. Atlantic yam/*Shan Yao*

PARTS USED *root and rhizome* TASTE *sweet*
CHARACTER *neutral* MERIDIANS *lung, spleen, kidney*
ACTIONS *relaxant for smooth muscles, antispasmodic, stimulates bile flow, anti-inflammatory, mild diaphoretic*

USES Atlantic yam *(D. villosa)* was the original source of the oral contraceptive pill, since it is rich in steroidal saponins. It is used largely for colic and rheumatism, but can also be taken for period pain, cramps, asthma, gastritis, and gall-bladder problems. It is very soothing for any spasmodic pain affecting smooth muscles. Wild yam is closely related to *Shan Yao (D. opposita)*, which is used in Chinese medicine to invigorate spleen and stomach energies and reinforce the lung and kidney. This also has a hormonal action and is believed to help *Jing* and strengthen the reproductive organs.

CAUTIONS Avoid in pregnancy.

MENTHA SPP. Peppermint/*Bo He*

PARTS USED *aerial parts, essential oil* TASTE *pungent*
CHARACTER *dry, generally cooling* MERIDIANS *lung, liver*
ACTIONS *antispasmodic, digestive tonic, anti-emetic, carminative, peripheral vasodilator, diaphoretic, bile stimulant, analgesic*

USES Peppermint *(Mentha x piperita)* has a high menthol content. It is a good carminative, relaxing the muscles of the digestive tract and stimulating bile flow. It is useful for indigestion, flatulence, colic, and so on, and is often combined with laxatives to prevent griping pains. It also reduces nausea. Its diaphoretic action is useful in fevers and flu. The Chinese use field mint *(Bo He, M. arvensis)* to clear chills associated with "wind-heat" and stimulate stagnant liver *Qi*.

CAUTIONS Avoid prolonged use of peppermint as it can irritate the mucous membranes; do not use the herb with children under four or the oil on those under ten.

NELUMBO NUCIFERA Lotus/*Lian*/*padma*

PARTS USED *seeds, root, leaves, leaf stem, receptacle/peduncle, stamens, plumule, rhizome node* TASTE *sweet, astringent* CHARACTER *neutral* MERIDIANS *heart, spleen, kidney* ACTIONS *astringent, stops bleeding, tonic, nervine*

USES The lotus has been used medicinally since ancient Egyptian times and in China almost all parts are used. The seeds (*Lian Zi*) are used mainly as a tonic for the spleen and stomach to combat diarrhea and stimulate the appetite. They are also a kidney tonic and calming sedative to ease insomnia and palpitations. In India the seeds are taken in powder with rice as a tonic for the heart and reproductive organs. They are believed to help the heart *chakra* and to encourage devotion and concentration, as well as improve speech and stammering. The root (*Lian Ou*) is used in ayurveda for root *chakra* disorders and in China to clear blood stasis. CAUTIONS Avoid in constipation and abdominal distension.

PIPER NIGRUM Black pepper/*Hu Jiao*/*marich*

PARTS USED *seeds* TASTE *pungent* CHARACTER *hot, dry* MERIDIANS *stomach, spleen, large intestine* ACTIONS *antiseptic, antibacterial, carminative, digestive and circulatory stimulant, topically rubefacient*

USES Black pepper is an effective warming stimulant for the digestive tract. It is a warm, dry plant and so was traditionally used in cooking to balance cold, damp vegetables such as beans, which tend to cause flatulence and stomach chills. In ayurveda it is used to energize *agni* and clear toxins from the digestive tract; it is also mixed with *ghee* for topical use on skin rashes. In China it is used mainly to warm the spleen and stomach, clear cold, and combat nausea, vomiting, and diarrhea associated with cold. CAUTIONS Avoid in "deficient *Yin*" and heat symptoms.

SANTALUM ALBA · Sandalwood/*chandana*

PARTS USED *wood, essential oil* **TASTE** *bitter, sweet, astringent* **CHARACTER** *cooling* **MERIDIANS** *spleen, heart, lung* **ACTIONS** *antiseptic, antibacterial, urinary antiseptic, carminative, relaxing, diuretic, antispasmodic, alterative*

USES Sandalwood is important in ayurvedic medicine as a cooling herb that calms the mind and improves digestive energy. It is also helpful for the circulation, respiration, and nervous system. Drops of the oil applied to the third eye (in the forehead) are said to relieve heat and thirst and reduce fevers, as well as encourage devotion and meditation. In Western aromatherapy the oil is regarded as relaxing and anti-depressant; it is used for urinary problems, nervous disorders, chest complaints, and to promote restful sleep.

CAUTIONS Avoid in high *kapha* conditions and severe lung congestion.

TRIGONELLA FOENUM-GRAECUM · Fenugreek/*Hu Lu Ba*/*methi*

PARTS USED *seeds* **TASTE** *pungent, bitter* **CHARACTER** *very warm* **MERIDIANS** *kidney* **ACTIONS** *antiparasitic, laxative, galactagogue*

USES Fenugreek is a very warming remedy, ideal for colds and chills affecting the abdomen. It is used in the West as a soothing, healing remedy for the stomach and intestines, helpful for colitis, diverticulitis, irritable bowel syndrome, weak digestion, and poor appetite. In ayurveda the plant is regarded as a good remedy in convalescence, helping to stimulate liver function and ease indigestion. The Chinese use *Hu Lu Ba* to warm the kidneys, dispel cold, and relieve pains in the abdomen and groin associated with kidney weakness.

CAUTIONS Avoid in pregnancy, if there are fire symptoms and in "deficient *Yin*."

OTHER HERBS THAT MAY BE HELPFUL
Dang Gui (p.173) ● *Ju Hua (p.64)* ● *Mu Dan Pi (p.175)*
● *curly dock (p.151)* ● *camomile (p.192)* ● *Atlantic yam (p.79)*
● *devil's claw (p.151)* ● *agrimony (p.192)* ● *sweet flag (p.51)*

Liver problems

**The liver is the largest organ in the body and in
orthodox anatomy is viewed as the body's
chemical factory—filtering the products of digestion
and converting useful chemicals into vital substances
needed for many body processes. The liver is also the
body's first line of defense, filtering and storing
potentially harmful substances to prevent them
entering the bloodstream and reaching the brain.**

*In our polluted world this inevitably means that our livers are coping
with pesticides, synthetic food additives, and the unknown effects of
genetically modified products. The resulting overload can lead to
congestion and poor liver function, so many Western herbalists routinely
include cleansing and tonifying liver herbs in their remedies to help this
overworked organ. Poor liver function may not only be related to obvious
digestive problems, such as constipation and
jaundice, but may also be a factor in skin
disorders, arthritic problems, and headaches.*

*In Chinese medicine the liver is classified with
the Zang organs and has a range of additional
attributes bearing little relation to Western concepts of
anatomy. It is believed to store blood and regulate its
release into the body as needed. This helps to
explain why the Chinese associate the liver with*

CURLY DOCK

RED WINE

the female menstrual cycle and often treat gynecological problems with liver tonics. The liver also regulates "Qi flow"—the way that this vital energy circulates through our bodies. The ideal is for a smooth, constant flow of Qi with no stagnation, which is believed to lead to dysfunction.

The liver is also said to "store the soul." This is one of the five aspects of the human spirit defined in Chinese theory and is the more ethereal component known as Hun, which is a little nearer to the Western concept of "soul" than the other form of "spirit."

Under the five-element model, the liver is also associated with the tendons, eyes, and nails, and with the emotion of anger. Aching tendons (generally most noticeable in the knees) can thus suggest liver imbalance, while strong, healthy pink nails suggest good liver Qi. Poor eyesight is seen as a result of "deficient liver blood," while irritant conditions such as conjunctivitis are defined in terms of heat or wind affecting the liver or liver meridians. Irritability and anger—often symptoms of PMS—are similarly blamed on liver imbalance.

FRINGETREE BARK

In ayurveda the liver is defined as a pitta, or fiery, organ— pitta literally translates as "bile"—and is thus the site of many pitta disorders, such as inflammations and infections; jaundice and hepatitis are seen as aggravated pitta conditions. The liver is also viewed as the focus of digestive energies and enzymes (bhuta agnis) and plays an important role in transforming the food we eat into the basic five elements (air, water, fire, earth, and ether), which ayurveda argues are then rebuilt into essential bodily substances. The liver is seen as the seat of fiery (pitta) emotions such as irritability, anger, jealousy, and ambition, as well as the more positive courage, enthusiasm, self-confidence, and determination.

BERBERIS SPP. Barberry/*daru haridra*

PARTS USED *stem bark, root bark, root* TASTE *bitter, pungent, astringent* CHARACTER *slightly warm, dry* MERIDIANS *spleen, stomach, liver, gall bladder* ACTIONS *liver stimulant, bile stimulant, alterative, antiseptic, anti-emetic, digestive tonic, hypotensive, mild sedative, febrifugal, anti-inflammatory, amebicidal, antibacterial, antidiarrheal*

USES *B. aristata* (*daru haridra* or "wood turmeric") is considered very similar in action to turmeric (p.130). The root is used as a cleansing remedy for skin problems and for diarrhea, jaundice, eye disease, and excessive menstrual bleeding. It is believed to destroy *ama* (toxins) and cleanse the liver. Western herbalists take a similar view of common barberry (*B. vulgaris*), using it mainly for liver congestion and in chronic skin problems. It stimulates bile flow and is a useful antiseptic for gastrointestinal infections.

CAUTIONS Avoid in pregnancy; do not take for more than four weeks without professional advice.

BUPLEURUM FALCATUM *Chai Hu*

PARTS USED *root* TASTE *bitter, pungent* CHARACTER *slightly cold* MERIDIANS *liver, gall bladder, pericardium, San Jiao* ACTIONS *antibacterial, antiviral, antimalarial, analgesic, anti-inflammatory, cholagogue, mild hypotensive, sedative*

USES Although *Chai Hu* is generally regarded as a remedy for fevers, malaria, and chills, it is also a potent liver herb and Western herbalists sometimes liken it to vervain. It is traditionally used to disperse wind and heat "evils," clear "stagnant liver *Qi*," and relieve depression. "Stagnant liver *Qi*" can be associated with menstrual problems as well as depression, and the herb is often included in remedies for PMS. *Chai Hu* is also given in cases of prolapse of the lower bowel or uterus associated with descending *Yang Qi*.

CAUTIONS Avoid in "liver fire" or "deficient *Yin*."

CHIONANTHUS VIRGINICUS — Fringetree

PARTS USED *root bark* TASTE *pungent, bitter, sweet*
CHARACTER *cool, dry* MERIDIANS *liver, gall bladder*
ACTIONS *liver stimulant, promotes bile flow, laxative, diuretic, alterative, tonic*

USES Fringetree is a traditional Native North American remedy, originally used for malaria and as a wound healer. It is now considered a highly effective liver and gall-bladder remedy for jaundice, gallstones, hepatitis, and poor liver function. It helps to liquefy bile and clear it from the system, as well as being useful for high blood pressure associated with congestion in the portal (liver) circulation. It is often combined in chronic liver conditions with barberry and Atlantic yam *(pp.84, 79)*, which eases spasmodic pain. The herb has a tonic action on the pancreas and has been used for excess sugar in the urine that is associated with diabetes.
CAUTIONS None noted.

LYCIUM BARBARUM/L. CHINENSE — Wolfberry/*Gou Qi Zi*

PARTS USED *fruit* TASTE *sweet* CHARACTER *neutral*
MERIDIANS *liver, kidney* ACTIONS *hypotensive, hypoglycemic, immune stimulant, liver tonic and restorative, reduces cholesterol levels*

USES Both Chinese wolfberry fruits and root bark *(Di Gu Pi)* are used in TCM, often in a traditional tonic wine combined with *Wu Wei Zi* for general debility. The herb is said to nourish liver and kidney *Yin* and blood, and "brighten the eyes." The berries are combined with *Ju Hua* for liver deficiency and, since the liver is closely related to the eyes, are also used in washes for poor eyesight. Porridge *(congee)* containing the berries is a popular home remedy for "kidney *Qi* deficiency," typified by impotence, low back pain, dizziness, and tinnitus.
CAUTIONS Avoid in excess heat syndromes and "deficient spleen with dampness."

PAEONIA LACTIFLORA White peony/*Bai Shao Yao*

PARTS USED *root* **TASTE** *sour, bitter* **CHARACTER** *slightly cold* **MERIDIANS** *liver, spleen* **ACTIONS** *antibacterial, anti-inflammatory, antispasmodic, diuretic, sedative, hypotensive, analgesic*

USES White peony is traditionally used in China to balance liver functions and energy, nourish the blood, "consolidate *Yin*," soothe liver *Qi*, and relieve pain. As a nourishing blood tonic, it figures in gynecological remedies. *Bai Shao* is sometimes roasted to reduce its cold nature or stir-fried to enhance its pain-relieving properties. It is used for a number of liver syndromes, including "ascending liver *Yang*" (typified by headaches and dizziness) and "disharmonies between spleen and liver" leading to digestive upsets, when it is often used with licorice. It is combined with *Dang Gui* for menstrual problems with liver or blood deficiency.
CAUTIONS Avoid in diarrhea and abdominal coldness.

SILYBUM MARIANUM Milk-thistle

PARTS USED *seeds* **TASTE** *bitter, pungent* **CHARACTER** *warm, dry* **MERIDIANS** *liver, heart* **ACTIONS** *bitter tonic, stimulates bile flow, antidepressant, antioxidant, antiviral, promotes milk flow*

USES Milk-thistle seeds are rich in silymarin, which research has identified as highly protective for the liver, helping to combat damage from pollutants and toxins. Extracts of silymarin have been used to treat cirrhosis and hepatitis; taking milk-thistle seeds helps prevent damaging the liver by alcohol abuse, reduces high cholesterol levels, and soothes gall-bladder inflammation. Milk-thistle is a more powerful antioxidant than vitamin E, so helps prevent damage to tissues by free radicals. The leaves are used in infusions to ease menstrual problems and stimulate milk flow in nursing mothers.
CAUTIONS None noted.

TARAXACUM SPP. Dandelion/*Pu Gong Ying*

PARTS USED *leaves, root* TASTE *sweet, bitter* CHARACTER *cold* MERIDIANS *liver, stomach* ACTIONS *leaves—diuretic, hepatic, and digestive tonic; root—liver tonic, stimulates bile flow, diuretic, laxative, antirheumatic*

USES In China the leaves of *Pu Gong Ying (Taraxacum mongolicum)* are used mainly to clear heat and toxins, as well as to treat damp-heat problems associated with the liver (typified by red, swollen eyes, and jaundice). In the West dandelion root *(T. officinale)* is preferred as a liver remedy that is cleansing and a mild laxative, and is often used in chronic skin problems and arthritis. The leaves are used mainly as a diuretic for problems associated with fluid retention and urinary dysfunction, although they also have a mild stimulating action on the liver. Dandelion is a comparative newcomer to Western herbalism, first mentioned in the fifteenth century.

CAUTIONS Avoid in severe diarrhea.

VERBENA OFFICINALIS Vervain/*Ma Bian Cao*

PARTS USED *aerial parts* TASTE *pungent, bitter* CHARACTER *cool* MERIDIANS *liver, spleen, urinary bladder* ACTIONS *relaxant tonic, stimulates milk production, diaphoretic, nervine, sedative, antispasmodic, hepatic restorative, laxative, uterine and bile stimulant*

USES Vervain was a sacred herb to the Romans and Druids. Today it is valued as a useful nervine and liver tonic. It is bitter and stimulating for the digestion and makes an ideal tonic in cases of convalescence and debility. Externally it can ease the pain of neuralgia. In Chinese medicine it is used as a cooling remedy in fevers and to clear toxins from abscesses. It also invigorates blood circulation and menstrual flow and is an anti-malarial and diuretic for urinary problems.

CAUTIONS Avoid in pregnancy, although it can be taken in labor to stimulate contractions.

OTHER HERBS THAT MAY BE HELPFUL
Dang Gui (p.173) ● *curly dock (p.151)* ● *barberry (p.84)*
● *dandelion (p.87)* ● *bilberry (p.97)*

DANDELION

Constipation

Western herbalists regard constipation as a

symptom rather than a disease syndrome and look

for underlying causes: diet, digestive weakness, or lifestyle issues.

Remedies may include irritant purgatives, but long-term use is generally

discouraged as these can result in conditions like diverticulitis. Chinese

theory usually blames excess heat for acute constipation, while chronic

problems are more often associated with either Yin deficiency or energy

weakness (common in the elderly). In ayurveda constipation is defined in

humoral terms: severe or chronic problems are generally vata-type. In

kapha-type constipation excess damp or mucus clogs the system.

CANNABIS SATIVA Marijuana/*Huo Ma Ren*

PARTS USED *seeds* TASTE *sweet* CHARACTER *neutral*
MERIDIANS *spleen, stomach, large intestine*
ACTIONS *laxative, hypotensive*

USES Cannabis is gradually being recognized in the
West as an important medicinal plant, used as an anti-
emetic and for the relief of muscular sclerosis, although
its use is still illegal in many countries. In China the
seeds are considered to be a gentle, moist laxative to
lubricate the intestines, nourish *Yin*, and clear heat.
They are a specific for constipation in the elderly, often
related to lack of energy and body fluids (*Jin-Ye*). Seeds
supplied by Western importers are usually boiled first to
prevent illicit cultivation. *Huo Ma Ren* is often combined
with *Dang Gui*, which is also a liver stimulant and laxative.
CAUTIONS Avoid in diarrhea.

PLANTAGO SPP. Isphagula/*snigdhajira*

PARTS USED *seeds, husks* TASTE *sweet, astringent*
CHARACTER *cool* MERIDIANS *large intestine*
ACTIONS *demulcent, bulking laxative, antidiarrheal*

USES Both isphagula *(P. ovata)* and closely related flea
seeds *(P. psyllium)* are widely used as bulking laxatives.
They are also prescribed by orthodox physicians for
irritable bowel syndrome, as the resulting bulky mass
can help to soothe diarrhea. Over-the-counter herbal
products often include the seeds in slimming aids, as
the bulky mass can fill the digestive tract and so reduce
hunger pangs. The seeds are similarly used in India,
where the plant originates, although as they can
deplete *agni* they are not recommended for long-term
use. Ginger or fennel may be added to combat
griping, and digestive stimulants to support *agni*.
CAUTIONS Always take capsules or dried isphagula
with plenty of water.

RHEUM PALMATUM Rhubarb/*Da Huang*/*amla vetasa*

PARTS USED *root, rhizome* TASTE *bitter* CHARACTER *cold*
MERIDIANS *liver, spleen, stomach, large intestine* ACTIONS
*purgative, antibacterial, antifungal, antiparasitic, hypotensive,
lowers blood cholesterol levels, cholagogue, diuretic, hemostatic*

USES In the West *Da Huang* is seen as rich in
anthraquinones—chemicals that irritate the gut and
encourage peristalsis. In China it is regarded primarily
as cooling, being used to drain heat and damp-heat,
clear "fire poisons"—*pitta* in ayurveda—and invigorate
blood circulation. It is used for fevers associated with
constipation and abdominal fullness, and for "heat in
the blood" where symptoms may include nosebleeds or
bleeding piles. As it clears "stagnant blood," *Da Huang*
may also be given for irregular or scanty menstruation.
CAUTIONS Avoid where there are no heat/fire symptoms.

OTHER HERBS THAT MAY BE HELPFUL
rhubarb (p.89) ● isphagula (p.89) ● agrimony (p.192)
● marigold (p.63) ● Jin Yin Hua (p.45) ● bilberry (p.97)
● rose (p.113) ● hawthorn (p.137)

AGRIMONY

Diarrhea

Like constipation, diarrhea is a symptom, not a
specific disease syndrome. In the West it may be
associated with self-limiting problems, such as
gastroenteritis, gastritis, or mild food poisoning, or be
a symptom of more chronic conditions, such as ulcerative
colitis or irritable bowel syndrome. An orthodox approach tends to regard
diarrhea as purely concerned with disorders of the digestive tract. While
many orthodox remedies are designed to stop the diarrhea, herbalists
tend to regard this as the body's way of removing toxins, so instead the
emphasis is on demulcent and astringent herbs to soothe inflamed tissues.

In Chinese medicine diarrhea is seen in terms of excess or deficiency:
excess is linked to damp-heat accumulating in the stomach/spleen and
large intestine and is similar to pitta-type diarrhea, to be treated with
cool, astringent herbs; deficient-type diarrhea is linked to Qi weakness or
Yang deficiency, usually in the kidney or spleen.

In ayurvedic medicine diarrhea commonly suggests dysentery and
infection. It is usually a pitta condition, when it is accompanied by fever,
thirst, and pus or blood in the stool; kapha-type diarrhea
would be similar to mucous colitis in the West, with
mucus in the stool and a lack of energy; vata-type
involves cramping pains and plenty of wind and
would include many of the symptoms labeled as
"irritable bowel syndrome" in the West.

ROSE BUDS

ATRACTYLODES CHINENSIS *Cang Zhu*

PARTS USED *rhizome* TASTE *pungent, bitter* CHARACTER *warm* MERIDIANS *spleen, stomach* ACTIONS *carminative, diaphoretic, increases excretion of sodium and potassium salts, although it is not diuretic*

USES Gray atractylodes, *Cang Zhu*, is one of the main Chinese herbs for clearing dampness—both for internal damp problems associated with spleen weakness and the *San Jiao* and for external damp. It also expels external wind and cold. It is used for problems like nausea, vomiting, indigestion, and diarrhea that are associated with damp in the spleen or *San Jiao*. It is also taken for arthritic problems and as a remedy for night blindness, often with sesame seeds (*Hei Zhi Ma*).

CAUTIONS Avoid in "deficient *Qi* or *Yin*" with interior heat.

MYRISTICA FRAGRANS Nutmeg/*Rou Dou Kou/jatiphala*

PARTS USED *seeds* TASTE *pungent* CHARACTER *warm* MERIDIANS *spleen, stomach, large intestine* ACTIONS *antispasmodic, anti-emetic, appetite stimulant, anti-inflammatory, carminative, digestive stimulant*

USES Nutmeg is familiar in the West as a kitchen seasoning, although it is also used medicinally, mainly for digestive upsets. In ayurveda it is believed to increase absorption in the small intestine and is taken in buttermilk to stop diarrhea and clear excess *vata* in the colon. It is also used to calm the mind. The Chinese use it as a warming digestive remedy for the spleen, stomach, and middle *Jiao*, to "restrain leakage from the intestines," stop diarrhea, and regulate *Qi* flow. It is also helpful for nausea, abdominal bloating, indigestion, and colic.

CAUTIONS Avoid in diarrhea caused by heat factors; large doses (7.5g or more in a single dose) may produce convulsions; avoid in pregnancy.

OTHER HERBS THAT MAY BE HELPFUL
ginger (p.185) ● camomile (p.192), ● lemon-balm (p.111)
● nutmeg (p.91) ● cloves (p.156) ● turmeric (p.130)
● fennel (p.65) ● peppermint (p.79)

CLOVES

Indigestion and bloating

Indigestion, with its associated heartburn, abdominal discomfort, and flatulence (wind), is usually blamed in the West on dietary deficiency, eating too fast, tight clothing, or stress. The orthodox approach is often simply to prescribe antacids, although herbalists take a more holistic approach, looking at diet and lifestyle, while using carminatives to soothe and normalize digestion.

In ayurvedic medicine indigestion is blamed on an accumulation of ama (toxins), caused by undigested food in the stomach and digestive tract. Associated symptoms are likely to include bad breath, abnormal appetite, and poorly formed stools. The ama ferment and eventually enter the bloodstream, being carried to other parts of the body, where they may lead to a range of chronic illnesses. Dismissing indigestion as a minor commonplace to be treated simply with antacids is—from the ayurvedic point of view—quite wrong, as the symptoms underlie a potentially serious health problem that needs to be resolved. This accumulation of undigested foods can further be classified as pitta, kapha, or vata, with appropriate treatment being given to prevent the ama from entering the bloodstream.

In Chinese medicine this concept of "food stagnation" is also very important and is explained more in terms of spleen and stomach Qi deficiency, with problems in processing foods and circulating fluids and water. As in ayurveda, it is seen as a potential long-term ailment that is likely to lead to chronic health problems if left untreated.

ELETTARIA CARDAMOMUM Cardamom/*ela*

PARTS USED *seeds* TASTE *pungent, sweet*
CHARACTER *heating* MERIDIANS *spleen, stomach,
kidney* ACTIONS *stimulant, expectorant, carminative,
stomachic, diaphoretic, appetite stimulant*

USES Cardamom seeds *(ela)* are a safe and effective
digestive stimulant to energize the spleen and kindle
agni. In ayurveda the herb is used to clear excess
kapha from the stomach and lungs and is believed to
stimulate the mind and heart, bringing clarity and joy.
In the West it is used mainly for wind and colic. The
Chinese use bastard cardamom *(Amomum
xanthioides)*, known as *Sha Ren*, mainly as an anti-
emetic to transform dampness, warm the spleen and
stomach, and move *Qi*. It is also used in pregnancy for
morning sickness and to help combat miscarriage.
CAUTIONS None noted for cardamom, but avoid *Sha
Ren* in "deficient *Yin*" with heat signs.

ULMUS RUBRA Slippery elm

PARTS USED *inner bark* TASTE *sweet, bland* CHARACTER *cool,
moist* MERIDIANS *lungs, stomach, urinary bladder*
ACTIONS *demulcent, emollient, laxative, nutritive, antitussive*

USES Slippery elm is a highly mucilaginous herb, used
mainly to coat the stomach and provide protection in
gastritis, heartburn, and ulceration. It may be taken to
combat travel sickness and is very soothing for
inflammatory problems in the lower bowel, such as
colitis and diverticulitis. Slippery elm is a valuable
nutrient, which can be made into a gruel with hot milk
and flavored with honey and spices for convalescents.
Externally it makes an effective drawing ointment for
splinters and boils and can soothe wounds and burns.
CAUTIONS None noted.

OTHER HERBS THAT MAY BE HELPFUL
echinacea (p.45) ● lemon-balm (p.111) ● Huang Qi (p.105) ● camomile (p.192) ● gotu kola (p.106) ● rosemary (p.71) ● ashwagandha (p.107) ● ginseng (p.106) ● aloe vera (p.63) ● thyme (p.43) ● marigold (p.63)

ECHINACEA

Candidiasis

Excess yeast in the digestive tract, generally due to the micro-organism Candida albicans, has been much publicized as a cause of health problems in recent years. Although hard medical evidence is scant, many alternative health-care practitioners blame a range of disorders—from panic attacks and neurosis to arthritic pains—on candidiasis.

The theory is that the excess yeasts take on a fungal form and burrow through the gut lining to enter the bloodstream, where the canditoxins that they produce can interfere with normal body chemistry and cause a wide diversity of symptoms. Strict anticandida diets are generally recommended, as well as antifungal supplements and Lactobacillus spp. (the "good" bacteria in the gut, which restore balance and destroy the excess yeasts causing the problem). Limited anticandida diets can in themselves weaken the system, reducing immunity and encouraging opportunist organisms like C. albicans to proliferate still further.

Sceptics regard candidiasis as a convenient label for symptoms related to weakened immune systems or food intolerance. In ayurveda it would be regarded as a result of weak agni, since the digestive fire should destroy invading toxins. The Chinese would explain it in terms of spleen Qi deficiency and excess phlegm. Energizing remedies, such as Huang Qi and ashwagandha, would be given to strengthen the immune system, as well as stomach and spleen remedies (see pp.78–81).

LEMON-BALM

FERULA ASSA-FOETIDA Asafetida/*E Wei/hingu*

PARTS USED *oleo gum resin* TASTE *pungent, bitter*
CHARACTER *warm* MERIDIANS *liver, spleen, stomach*
ACTIONS *carminative, expectorant, antifungal, anthelmintic, stimulant, aphrodisiac, analgesic*

USES Asafetida (or devil's dung) is a potent digestive remedy, used in ayurveda to clear food stagnation from the digestive tract and strengthen *agni*. It cleanses and normalizes the gut flora, so can be helpful in candidiasis. It clears parasitic roundworms and threadworms and relieves excess wind and abdominal bloating due to a surfeit of *vata*. Externally asafetida paste is used on arthritic joints and for abdominal pain. In the West it is used mainly to clear mucus and phlegm in bronchitis, asthma, and whooping cough, while the Chinese use it for food stagnation.

CAUTIONS Avoid in young children and babies, in pregnancy or severe spleen weakness.

TABEBUIA IMPETIGINOSA

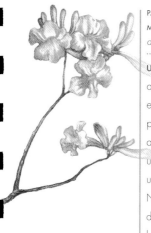

PARTS USED *inner bark* TASTE *bitter* CHARACTER *cooling*
MERIDIANS *stomach* ACTIONS *antitumor, antimicrobial, anti-fungal, analgesic, diuretic, anti-inflammatory*

USES This herb has been recognized as antitumor and antifungal since the 1860s, and recent studies suggest effectiveness against various cancers. It is widely promoted in the West as an anticandida remedy, but is also effective for colds, flu, and fevers. It is used for ulcers, rheumatism, high blood pressure, skin infections, urinary inflammations, and pelvic inflammatory disease. Native South Americans traditionally took it in a decoction, but studies suggest that finely powdered bark in capsules is more effective.

CAUTIONS High doses (4–6g) may cause nausea and are best avoided by those taking anticoagulant drugs.

OTHER HERBS THAT MAY BE HELPFUL
turmeric (p.130) ● garlic (p.128) ● ginseng (p.106) ● bladderwrack
(p.150) ● stinging nettle (p.71) ● camomile (p.192) ● dandelion
(p.87) ● hops (p.115) ● licorice (p.41) ● betony (p.121)

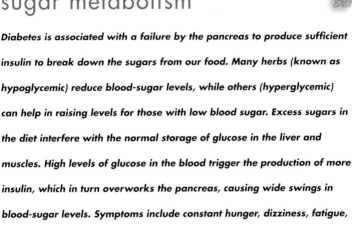

SUGAR

Diabetes and sugar metabolism

Diabetes is associated with a failure by the pancreas to produce sufficient insulin to break down the sugars from our food. Many herbs (known as hypoglycemic) reduce blood-sugar levels, while others (hyperglycemic) can help in raising levels for those with low blood sugar. Excess sugars in the diet interfere with the normal storage of glucose in the liver and muscles. High levels of glucose in the blood trigger the production of more insulin, which in turn overworks the pancreas, causing wide swings in blood-sugar levels. Symptoms include constant hunger, dizziness, fatigue, headaches, irritability, memory lapses, visual disturbances, panic attacks, and twitching limbs. Eating sweet food generally brings rapid relief.

In ayurveda, diabetes—with its symptoms of thirst and excess urination —is seen as a water problem related mainly to kapha. It is classified initially as a kapha problem but, if untreated, leads to tissue-wasting and therefore becomes more vata in character. Turmeric is often used to help regulate pancreatic function in the early stages of the illness.

The Chinese similarly associate diabetes with water metabolism, often classifying it as a symptom of kidney Yin deficiency, to be treated with energizing tonic herbs.

TYPES OF DIABETES

Juvenile onset diabetes is often hereditary and leads to insulin dependence, which always requires professional treatment. The late-onset variety—usually starting in the sixties or seventies— is regarded by Western herbalists as the result of a lifetime of poor diet, with too many sugars and an irregular pattern of meals.

ARTEMISIA ABSINTHIUM   Wormwood

PARTS USED *aerial parts* TASTE *very bitter, pungent, astringent* CHARACTER *cold, dry* MERIDIANS *stomach, spleen, lung* ACTIONS *bitter digestive tonic, stimulant, anthelmintic, anti-inflammatory, carminative, bile stimulant*

USES A bitter herb to activate the digestion, wormwood also clears liver and gall-bladder congestion and may be helpful to combat travel sickness. By stimulating digestion, it helps to normalize sugar metabolism, so one or two drops of tincture on the tongue make an ideal alternative to chocolate bars, which are usually munched by those suffering from low blood-sugar levels. Wormwood once formed the key flavoring in absinthe, which was a popular drink in the nineteenth century (now banned because of its toxicity). Fresh, pressed juices and infusions are safe.

CAUTIONS Contains thujone, which is a toxic and addictive hallucinogen, so it should be used only for short periods; avoid in pregnancy and epilepsy.

VACCINIUM MYRTILLUS   Bilberry

PARTS USED *leaves, fruit* TASTE *astringent, sour* CHARACTER *cold, dry* MERIDIANS *stomach, spleen, lung* ACTIONS *astringent, hypoglycemic, tonic, antiseptic, anti-emetic*

USES Bilberry fruits are a good source of vitamin C, highly astringent and antibacterial. They are used for diarrhea and colitis, but in large quantities have the opposite effect, so are good for constipation. The fruits have been used externally in salves for piles, burns, and skin complaints, as well as in mouthwashes for bleeding gums. The leaves reduce blood-sugar levels and may encourage insulin production and tonify the pancreas.

CAUTIONS The leaves should be avoided by insulin-dependent diabetics unless under professional guidance.

Holistic health tips

• In traditional health theories, the food we eat not only provides essential nutrients but, like medicinal herbs, can have a direct effect on our health and well-being. Just as herbs can be hot or cold, warm or dry to balance inner disharmonies, so too with foods.

• In Galenic theory eating "cold" foods in summer and "warm" foods in winter helped to balance the effect of a seasonal climate. In contrast, in the East where temperatures can be more extreme, "cold" foods were encouraged in winter to bring the body into harmony with its surroundings, while "hot" spicy foods were the preferred choice in summer when temperatures soared. For temperate, maritime climates a Galenic approach would be more logical, while those living with sub-tropical, continental extremes might prefer the Eastern approach.

• "Warm" and "hot" foods include: almonds, brown sugar, cherries, chicken, chives, dates, garlic, ginger, green and red bell peppers, green onions, ham, kumquats, leeks, lentils, mint, mustard and cress, mustard, mutton, onions, peaches, pepper, raspberries, rocket, shrimp, sorrel, soybean oil, sunflower seeds, walnuts, wine.

• "Cool" and "cold" foods include: apples, bamboo shoots, bananas, button mushrooms, clams, crab, cucumbers, endive, grapefruit, lettuce, mangoes, mung beans, pears, persimmons, purslane, seaweed, strawberries, tofu, tomatoes, water chestnuts, watercress, water melons.

• Neutral foods include: apricots, beef, beet, Chinese leaves, carrots, celery, maize, eggs, honey, polished white rice, potatoes, pumpkins, white sugar.

THE EMOTIONS
Western Approach

Above *Western orthodox medicine focuses on pills to ease symptoms rather than treat the whole person.*

For the past 300 years or so we in the West have tended to divide the spiritual and physical aspects of life into two quite separate categories—an approach said to originate with the French philosopher René Descartes (1596–1650), who argued that intangibles like religious faith have no place in the physical world.

This separation means that illness is largely defined purely in terms of pathology, rather than in relation to the whole person and his or her emotional or spiritual well-being. The closest orthodox practitioners come to evoking a non-physical factor in illness is to blame our ills on "stress" and offer antidepressants.

Stress *(see pp.108–9)* can have a physical effect on the body by producing additional supplies of the hormone adrenalin—the "fight or flight" hormone that helps prepare the body for action. This so-called "adrenalin rush" can create a euphoric "high," which some find addictive. Calming herbs and relaxation techniques may be used to combat the body's need for that potent adrenalin rush, thus reducing the likelihood of springing into "panic mode" without due cause. The Western herbal repertoire includes a great many

Below *Fighting or taking flight is not considered an appropriate response to stress in the office.*

nervines, which soothe and restore the nervous system to encourage greater relaxation and restful sleep, as well as others that can help to raise the stress threshold so that the damaging "flight or fight" response is reserved for real crises.

There are also a number of stimulating remedies to help strengthen what Victorian herbalists described as "the vital force" and boost energy levels to combat exhaustion.

THE EMOTIONS
Chinese Approach

Below *The ritual dancing of Buddhist monks calms the emotions and helps to sustain the spirit.*

TCM pays little attention to the nervous and stress-related problems that preoccupy the West, which in part reflects the static nature of the society in which it developed. However, emotional imbalance is seen as a very real cause of internal disease, with excess of any of the emotions linked to the *Zang-Fu* organs (grief, sadness, fear, anger, worry, joy, or fright) likely to lead to an imbalance in the physical organ as well. "Joy" is difficult for Westerners to link with illness and is better translated as "inappropriate behavior" (as in a mania) linked with anxiety.

Chinese medicine is also rich in energizing tonic remedies to strengthen the fundamental substances (*see p.17*) of *Qi*, *Jing*, and *Shen*. Early Chinese medicine was closely linked with religion, so there is a strong underlying spiritual dimension that is largely lacking in Western orthodox medicine. Herbs may be used to affect not only the emotions associated with the *Zang-Fu* organs, but also the five related aspects of the soul:

Below *Meditation is a calming exercise for the mind, with noticeable benefits for the body.*

- *Yi* (linked to the spleen)—sometimes described as thought or the "consciousness of possibilities."
- *Hun* (liver)—the ethereal, non-corporal soul.
- *Zhi* (kidney)—usually translated as "will" but also closely associated with wisdom or faith.
- *Po* (lungs)—the corporal or animal soul, closely linked with the emotions.
- *Shen* (heart)—the spirit, subtly different from the fundamental substance *Shen*; associated more with formal behavior.

THE EMOTIONS
Ayurvedic Approach

Like Chinese medicine, ayurveda derives from a time when religion and healing were synonymous and when the holistic nature of our being was taken for granted. In ancient India two fundamental principles were believed to lie behind all existence: *purusha* (the primal spirit) and *prakruti* (the great nature). Their union, combining spirit and matter, produced not only all things, but also *mahat*—the cosmic intelligence that is awakened in those who achieve buddhahood.

Above *Green stones (jade and peridot) are helpful for nervous function and nerve pains.*

Prakruti is identified with the three *gunas (see p.22)* of *sattva, rajas,* and *tamas.* Of these, *sattva* is the most desirable, being associated with truth, humility, honesty, and the general good. *Sattvic* herbs and foods help to encourage this quality. *Rajasic* and *tamasic* foods and herbs are also needed to maintain balance, but the *sattvic* remedies are most important as they awaken the mind and strengthen the spirit.

Above *Yellow stones (topaz and citrine) help to ease emotional problems that are associated with hormonal imbalance.*

Emotional or mental problems are related to imbalance in the *gunas* and *doshas* (humors), while the physical nervous system is also closely associated with both. Nerve impulses themselves belong to *vata*, so *vata* disorders always involve some sort of weakness or hypersensitivity in the nervous system and are called *vatavyadhi* or *vata* diseases. High *pitta* can also burn the nervous system, while excess *kapha* (phlegm) can clog and slow it. Also relevant is the *prana* (breath) flow through the body—if its movement is blocked, then there may be numbness, tremors, or spasms.

Above *Pearl and silver are linked to the moon and are believed to be calming and nurturing for the mind.*

Ayurveda also recommends gem treatments for energy and emotional imbalances: usually wearing a ring or other jewelry with the appropriate stone.

Above *Gold is stimulating and restorative.*

101

OTHER HERBS THAT MAY BE HELPFUL
lavender (p.141) ● rose (p.113) ● gotu kola (p.106)
● camomile (p.192) ● sweet flag (p.51) ● betony (p.121)
● rosemary (p.71)

Anxiety and tension headaches

Tension headaches usually start with a tightening of the muscles at the back of the neck and then creep forward until the whole head feels painful. Western practitioners link them to stress or muscle strain in the shoulders and neck, from sitting or working awkwardly, perhaps hunched over a desk or computer keyboard. Treatment can involve massage using soothing oils, such as lavender, across the neck or temples, as well as the internal use of relaxing nervines, such as skullcap and valerian, to ease tension and general anxiety states.

In TCM headaches are defined in terms of Zang-Fu imbalance or external factors. Practitioners look for associated symptoms that pinpoint the problem: dizziness and ringing in the ears, for example, may suggest a kidney deficiency syndrome. The kidneys are associated with the emotion of fear, which may also play a part in anxiety problems.

Headaches linked to anxiety are seen in ayurveda as vata problems and may be associated with dry skin, irregular diet, excessive activity, and constipation. Sedating herbs and purgatives are likely to be used. Pitta headaches are more likely to be associated with irritability and anger and may be treated with liver herbs such as gotu kola. Anxiety and stress are believed to damage ojas—the essential vigor or energy of the body—so supporting tonic herbs, such as shatavari or ashwagandha, may be added in chronic conditions.

SCUTELLÁRIA LATERIFLORA   Blue skullcap

PARTS USED *aerial parts*   TASTE *bitter, astringent*
CHARACTER *cold, dry*   MERIDIANS *heart, kidney*
ACTIONS *relaxing and restorative nervine, antispasmodic, bitter*

USES The variety of skullcap most widely used in Western medicine originates from Virginia and was introduced to Europe as a treatment for rabies—hence the alternative name of "mad dog herb." Today it is used as a relaxing sedative for stress and anxiety, although in the past it was used for jaundice, urinary-tract infections, hemorrhage, and threatened miscarriage. The herb helps to circulate *Qi* to clear energy constraint, which may be associated with anxiety and pain, and is helpful for nervous exhaustion, insomnia, and palpitations with heart or kidney energy deficiency.
CAUTIONS None noted.

VALERIANA OFFICINALIS   Valerian/*tagara*

PARTS USED *root, rhizome*   TASTE *bitter, pungent*
CHARACTER *warm, dry*   MERIDIANS *heart, pericardium, lung, spleen*   ACTIONS *tranquilizer, antispasmodic, expectorant, diuretic, hypotensive, carminative, mild anodyne*

USES Valerian is helpful for all sorts of nervous tension, blood-pressure problems related to stress, migraines, overexcitability in children, tension headaches, menopausal problems, anxiety associated with PMS, and sleeplessness. It will also help ease period pains, muscle cramps, and palpitations. Extracts are sometimes used in skin creams for stress-related eczema. *V officinalis* and a related species (*V. hardwickii*)—both known as *tagara*—are used in ayurveda for *vata*-related nervous problems; it is also used for vertigo, fainting, and hysteria.
CAUTIONS Excess doses (more than 5g) may cause headaches; do not combine with sleeping tablets.

OTHER HERBS THAT MAY BE HELPFUL
rosemary (p.71) ● basil (p.117) ● Siberian ginseng (p.109)
● turmeric (p.130) ● oats (p.109) ● Dang Shen (p.119)

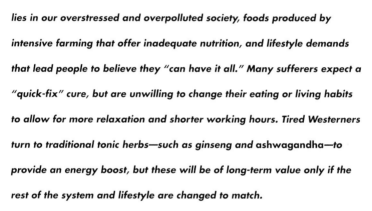

GINSENG

Fatigue and lack of energy

Constant tiredness is one of the most common

complaints that any Western practitioner hears from

his or her patients. Part of the problem undoubtedly

lies in our overstressed and overpolluted society, foods produced by

intensive farming that offer inadequate nutrition, and lifestyle demands

that lead people to believe they "can have it all." Many sufferers expect a

"quick-fix" cure, but are unwilling to change their eating or living habits

to allow for more relaxation and shorter working hours. Tired Westerners

turn to traditional tonic herbs—such as ginseng and ashwagandha—to

provide an energy boost, but these will be of long-term value only if the

rest of the system and lifestyle are changed to match.

Chinese medicine reserves the powerful tonic remedies for obvious

Qi- or Jing-deficiency syndromes, rather than using them as a convenient

energy top-up. Qi weakness is also likely to need the additional help of

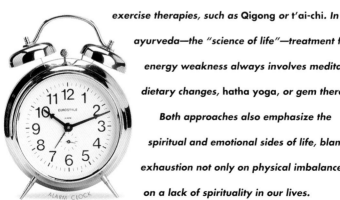

exercise therapies, such as Qigong or t'ai-chi. In

ayurveda—the "science of life"—treatment for

energy weakness always involves meditation,

dietary changes, hatha yoga, or gem therapy.

Both approaches also emphasize the

spiritual and emotional sides of life, blaming

exhaustion not only on physical imbalance but

on a lack of spirituality in our lives.

ALARM CLOCK

ASPARAGUS RACEMOSUS Asian asparagus/*Tian Men Dong*/*shatavari*

PARTS USED *root* TASTE *bitter, sweet* CHARACTER *cool* MERIDIANS *lung, kidney* ACTIONS *tonic, demulcent, antibacterial, antitussive, expectorant, antitumor*

USES Asian asparagus is one of ayurveda's most important tonics. It is used for any debility associated with the female sexual organs, but is also regarded as a soothing demulcent for the digestive and respiratory systems, being used for dry coughs, fevers with thirst, pleurisy, sunstroke, and for inflammatory digestive problems such as dysentery. In China the roots are mainly used to nourish *Yin* and clear heat. It is given for symptoms of kidney energy weakness, such as night sweats, as well as to replenish body fluids.

CAUTIONS Traditionally *Tian Men Dong* is avoided in diarrhea and in coughs caused by common colds.

ASTRAGALUS MEMBRANACEUS *Huang Qi*

PARTS USED *root* TASTE *sweet* CHARACTER *slightly warm* MERIDIANS *spleen, lung* ACTIONS *antispasmodic, diuretic, cholagogue, antibacterial, hypoglycemic, nervous stimulant, hypotensive, immune stimulant*

USES *Huang Qi* is an important *Qi* tonic often used for younger people, while *Ren Shen* was considered better for the over-40s. It also tonifies blood, stabilizes *Wei Qi* (defense energy), regulates water metabolism, and is a useful antibacterial to clear pus and encourage wound healing. It is often used for deficient spleen syndromes presenting as poor appetite, tiredness, and diarrhea, as well as for weakened *Wei Qi* typified by recurrent infections or respiratory problems. It is taken after childbirth to help restore *Qi* and blood.

CAUTIONS Avoid in excess *(Shi)* syndromes or if there is "deficient *Yin*."

CENTELLA ASIATICA   Indian pennywort/*gotu kola*

PARTS USED *aerial parts* **TASTE** *bitter* **CHARACTER** *cooling*
MERIDIANS *kidney, spleen* **ACTIONS** *rejuvenative tonic, cooling in fevers, immune stimulant, cleansing, bitter digestive stimulant, laxative, sedative*

USES The Sanskrit name for *gotu kola* is *brahmi*, as it is believed to increase knowledge of *Brahman*, the supreme reality. It is one of the most important *rasayanas* (longevity tonics) in ayurveda, helping to revitalize the brain and nervous system, combat aging and senility, and improve the memory. It is a specific tonic for *pitta*, while clearing excess *vata* and *kapha*; it is calming, *sattvic*, and an important aid for spiritual renewal. In the West it is used for digestive and nervous problems and as a skin cleansing remedy.
CAUTIONS Avoid in pregnancy and epilepsy; do not use for more than six weeks without a break.

PANAX GINSENG   Ginseng/*Ren Shen*

PARTS USED *root* **TASTE** *sweet, slightly bitter* **CHARACTER** *warm*
MERIDIANS *spleen, lung, heart* **ACTIONS** *tonic, stimulant, hypoglycemic, reduces cholesterol levels, immunostimulant*

USES Ginseng is China's most important *Qi* tonic. It has been extensively researched and is known to be rich in steroidal compounds that are very similar to human sex hormones—hence its reputation as an aphrodisiac. The herb also tonifies spleen and lung, generates body fluids, benefits heart *Qi*, and calms *Shen* (spirit). It is a powerful all-round tonic, helping the body adapt to stressful situations, restore energy, and combat chronic weaknesses. It is particularly good for the elderly. As a general tonic, it is ideally taken for one month in late fall when the seasons change from *Yang* to *Yin*.
CAUTIONS Avoid in heat conditions and "deficient *Yin*."

PANAX QUINQUEFOLIUS American ginseng/*Xi Yang Shen*

PARTS USED *root* TASTE *sweet, slightly bitter* CHARACTER *cool* MERIDIANS *heart, lung, kidney* ACTIONS *cardiotonic, hormonal action, sedative*

USES American ginseng was "discovered" by Jesuit priests in Canada in the early eighteenth century. It was classified as a gentler, more *Yin* remedy than the native Korean ginseng and is used mainly to nourish *Qi*, fluids and lung *Yin*. In China it is used for chronic coughs associated with lung deficiency (as in tuberculosis) and with low-grade fevers. It is also employed as a gentle energy tonic for fatigue and debility in chronic disorders and convalescence, when a stronger *Yang* tonic would be inappropriate.

CAUTIONS Avoid where there are symptoms of cold and damp in the stomach.

WITHANIA SOMNIFERA *ashwagandha*

PARTS USED *root* TASTE *bitter, astringent, sweet* CHARACTER *heating* MERIDIANS *kidney, lung* ACTIONS *tonic, nervine, sedative, anti-inflammatory, antitumor, aphrodisiac*

USES *Ashwagandha* is sometimes called "Indian ginseng" and is an important ayurvedic tonic, believed to increase vitality and clear the mind. Its traditional reputation as an aphrodisiac has been confirmed in clinical trials. In the West it is used mainly as a tonic for the elderly and to combat debility resulting from overwork and chronic stress. In India it is also used as a tonic in pregnancy and to encourage healthy growth in children. Studies have shown that the herb may slow the development of lung cancers in animals and regress tumors. *Ashwagandha* can also nourish the blood, improving hemoglobin levels in anemia.

CAUTIONS Avoid in high *ama* conditions.

OTHER HERBS THAT MAY BE HELPFUL
lemon-balm (p.111) ● *St.-John's-wort (p.111)*
● *valerian (p.103)* ● *turmeric (p.130)* ● *basil (p.117)*

LEMON-BALM

Stress

Stress is a normal and necessary part of our lives, providing a stimulus for activity and invention. Our bodies are equipped to deal with it—our hormonal system springs into action to give us the energy for "flight or fight" (see box). Stress is part of being alive—without it we cease to function.

That "flight or fight" response is fine if we can do either of these actions, but if we can't, then the body remains overactive, in a constant state of alertness, adding to feelings of frustration and a sense of being overloaded. This is what is commonly labeled "stress" but which is more accurately the "negative stress response." If this response gets out of hand, it can be extremely damaging to our health and can increase the risk of a wide range of life-threatening diseases.

Negative stress is less common in traditional societies where people naturally behave more intuitively and are faced with fewer stressful factors or difficult decisions affecting their mental well-being than those of us who live in the developed world. "Stresses" in the days of the early ayurvedic or Taoist practitioners were generally ones where "fight or flight" would have been an appropriate reaction, whereas in modern society punching a demanding superior on the nose or running out of the office when the going gets tough are rather less viable options.

FIGHT OR FLIGHT?
This response occurs in stressful situations, when adrenalin pours into the body to help it cope; the resulting adrenalin rush can provide a "high" that is potentially addictive.

AVENA SATIVA Oats

PARTS USED *seeds, straw, bran, whole unripe plant* TASTE *sweet* CHARACTER *warm, moist* MERIDIANS *spleen, kidney* ACTIONS *antidepressant, restorative nerve tonic, diaphoretic, nutritive; oatbran—antithrombotic, reduces cholesterol levels*

USES Oats have been used as a staple food in northern Europe for centuries. The plant is a nourishing and restorative tonic for blood, *Jing*, and *Qi*, and is good for liver and kidney weakness. It is an effective nerve tonic, especially for exhaustion associated with overwork, aging, anemia, and chronic illness. It also helps to circulate *Qi* and reduce tension. More recently it has been shown to reduce blood-cholesterol levels. Externally oatmeal is often used in skin remedies, while oat straw was a medieval remedy for rheumatism.

CAUTIONS Use with care in cases of gluten sensitivity (celiac disease).

ELEUTHEROCOCCUS SENTICOSUS Siberian ginseng/*Wu Jia Pi*

PARTS USED *root, root bark* TASTE *pungent* CHARACTER *warm* MERIDIANS *liver, kidney* ACTIONS *combats stress, antiviral, aphrodisiac, immune and circulatory stimulant, regulates blood pressure, hypoglycemic, adrenal stimulant*

USES Although *Wu Jia Pi* (root bark) has been used in TCM for 2,000 years, this herb was "rediscovered" in the West in the 1950s, then used extensively by Soviet athletes to increase stamina. It helps the body to cope with increased stress levels and improves concentration and mental activity. It is usually regarded as gentler in action than Korean ginseng and may be a preferred choice for women. In China the bark of the root is used to clear dampness and smooth *Qi* and blood flows. It is especially suitable for the elderly.

CAUTIONS Use *Wu Jia Pi* with caution in "deficient *Yin* with heat signs" (i.e. chronic debility).

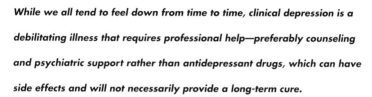

OTHER HERBS THAT MAY BE HELPFUL
oats (p.109) ● vervain (p.87) ● camomile (p.192)
● rosemary (p.71) ● basil (p.117)

BASIL

Depression

While we all tend to feel down from time to time, clinical depression is a debilitating illness that requires professional help—preferably counseling and psychiatric support rather than antidepressant drugs, which can have side effects and will not necessarily provide a long-term cure.

In traditional Galenic medicine depression was regarded as "melancholia" and was considered to be the result of too much "black bile" in the system. This excess would be treated with strong purgatives and digestive remedies to cleanse the system. Chronic depression is often accompanied by constipation, as intense sadness seems to shut down the digestive system, so the therapy may not have been as inappropriate as it sounds today. Modern herbal medicine uses many of the traditional herbs for melancholia, which have now been relabeled as antidepressants, although this rarely includes the once-popular strong purgatives.

In Chinese medicine depression is generally seen as a symptom of spleen imbalance, with the spleen's associated emotion—worry— interfering with its role of transporting nutrients and water through the body. This leads to Qi stagnation with symptoms of depression, poor appetite, restless sleep, forgetfulness and palpitations.

Ayurveda also views chronic depression—as it does other mental problems—as a whole-body syndrome, which may be associated with spiritual factors or damage to sattva, through excess tamas leading to apathy, inertia, and delusion. Treatment involves meditation and yoga as well as sattvic remedies and diet.

HYPERICUM PERFORATUM St.-John's-wort

PARTS USED *flowering tops, leaves* TASTE *bitter, sweet, astringent* CHARACTER *cool, dry* MERIDIANS *lung, kidney, urinary bladder* ACTIONS *astringent, analgesic, anti-inflammatory, sedative, restoring nerve tonic, antidepressant, antispasmodic, antiviral*

USES Although a traditional wound healer, St.-John's-wort is now better known as an antidepressant. The herb has been successfully used in seasonal affective disorder, for emotional upsets in the menopause, and in mild cases of depression. It is also used for PMS, period pains, and in AIDS therapy. Externally, infused St-John's-wort oil is ideal for minor wounds and burns.

CAUTIONS Research suggests that excessively high doses (up to fifty times the typical dose of 2–4g) may be linked to cataracts and there are concerns over possible interactions with prescription drugs; prolonged use may increase the photosensitivity of the skin.

MELISSA OFFICINALIS Lemon-balm

PARTS USED *aerial parts, essential oil* TASTE *bitter, astringent, sour* CHARACTER *cold, dry* MERIDIANS *heart, San Jiao, lung, liver, pericardium* ACTIONS *sedative, antidepressant, digestive stimulant, peripheral vasodilator, diaphoretic, relaxing restorative for nervous system, antiviral, antibacterial*

USES Lemon-balm is a cool, gentle herb useful for treating a wide range of ailments—from nervous stomach upsets in children to depression, anxiety, and tension headaches. The plant is sedating for heart fire and calms liver *Yang*, which can cause headaches and eye problems. It is also useful for period pains and feverish infections, including mumps, chicken pox, and shingles. Externally, lemon-balm creams can be used on insect bites, sores, and slow-healing wounds.

CAUTIONS None noted.

OTHER HERBS THAT MAY BE HELPFUL
St-John's-wort (p.111) ● betony (p.121)
● camomile (p.192) ● vervain (p.87) ● camphor (p.157)

CAMPHOR

Emotional upsets

Modern medicine tends to leave emotional problems to

psychologists and counselors. However, like their Chinese and ayurvedic

counterparts, Western herbalists regard such conditions as more closely

intertwined with physical well-being. Today flower remedies—those

discovered by Dr. Edward Bach (1886–1936) or the newer Bush essences

or Quintessentials—are used to promote emotional well-being. Chinese

tradition closely links the emotions to specific Zang-Fu organs, with

imbalance in the body blamed for emotional instability. In ayurveda, too,

it is impossible to separate emotional well-being from the whole person.

Herbs may be used to strengthen the chakras linked with the mind.

ARTEMISIA VULGARIS   Mugwort/*Ai Ye*/*nagadamani*

PARTS USED *leaves* TASTE *pungent, bitter* CHARACTER *warm*
MERIDIANS *lung, liver, spleen, kidney* ACTIONS *antibacterial,
antifungal, bitter digestive tonic, expectorant, uterine stimulant,
anthelmintic, carminative, antiseptic*

USES Mugwort was once associated with magic. It is
used for menstrual problems, especially with nervous
tension, and is a calming remedy for emotional upsets
at the menopause. In China it is the *moxa* used for
moxabustion treatments and is a warming remedy for
the meridians, to stop bleeding, dispel cold, and clear
phlegm. It is also used for threatened miscarriage and
infertility. It may also be effective for malaria.
CAUTIONS Avoid in epilepsy, heat in the blood caused
by "deficient *Yin*" or high *pitta* conditions; use in
pregnancy under professional guidance only.

ROSA SPP. Rose/*Jin Ying Zi/Mei Gui Hua/shatapatri*

PARTS USED *petals, hips* **TASTE** *sweet, astringent* **CHARACTER** *neutral, cooling, or slightly warming (varies with species)* **MERIDIANS** *kidney, urinary bladder, large intestine, liver, spleen* **ACTIONS** *antidepressant, antispasmodic, astringent, antibacterial, antiviral, reduces cholesterol levels, tonifies uterus, sedative, digestive stimulant, increases bile production, expectorant, kidney tonic, blood tonic, menstrual regulator*

USES All sorts of roses feature in Western, Chinese, and ayurvedic medicine. In Europe the damask rose (*R. damascena*) is the source of rose oil used in aromatherapy for depression, anxiety, as an aphrodisiac, and for those lacking love, while dog rose (*R. canina*) has been used since Roman times as an astringent wound healer. Traditionally roses are said to be good for the "skin and the soul." The petals are also helpful in panic attacks, neuroses, and digestive problems. In China Cherokee rosehips (*Jin Ying Zi—R. laevigata*) and Japanese rosebuds (*Mei Gui Hua—R. rugosa*) are both used, although their actions are quite different. *Mei Gui Hua* is more warming and a *Qi* and blood tonic for the liver, while *Jin Ying Zi* is focused on the kidney and *Jing*, so it is used for treating urinary problems, as well as impotence and premature ejaculation. In ayurveda many types of roses are used as healing remedies for eye and digestive problems, while *shatapatri* (*R. damascena*) petals are made into a conserve with sugar as a tonic remedy. All members of the species are astringent and can be helpful for sore throats, diarrhea, and inflamed surfaces.

CAUTIONS Avoid *Jin Ying Zi* in excess fire and heat syndromes; use species rose only—garden cultivars may show other properties; rose oil is very expensive and is often contaminated with synthetic adulterants.

113

OTHER HERBS THAT MAY BE HELPFUL
lavender (p.141) ● *St.-John's-wort (p.111)* ● *camomile (p.192)*
● *betony (p.121)* ● *lemon-balm (p.111)*
● *pasque flower (p.187)* ● *longan (p.120)*

Insomnia

There is a Chinese saying that a woman needs six hours' sleep, a man seven, and only a fool needs eight. Few would wholeheartedly agree with this theory, but it is certainly true that the amount of sleep that each of us needs varies considerably and that at some times we need rather more sleep than we do at others.

Sleeplessness becomes a problem only when sufferers feel tired and unable to concentrate during the day or when it becomes a worry in itself, with seemingly endless hours spent tossing in bed at night. In general the body will eventually catch up and a few bad nights are generally followed by a period of restful, restorative sleep.

Western medicine looks to causes such as heavy meals late at night, leading to disturbed digestion; painful joints and muscles; or irritating coughs, which keep people awake. Insomnia can also be associated with tension and worries and with a failure to relax before bedtime.

*In Chinese theory **Qi** moves around the body during the 24-hour day, so waking at a particular time is associated with an imbalance in a certain organ, and this guides treatment.*

In ayurvedic theory insomnia is associated with vata affecting the nervous system and is likely to be accompanied by frightening dreams, worry, and a lack of "groundedness"—common in excess vata problems where the earth element is weak.

BETONY

ST.-JOHN'S-WORT

HUMULUS LUPULUS Hops

PARTS USED *strobiles* TASTE *bitter, astringent, pungent* CHARACTER *cold, dry* MERIDIANS *heart, pericardium, kidney, liver* ACTIONS *sedative, anaphrodisiac, restoring tonic for the nervous system, bitter digestive stimulant, diuretic*

USES Hops have been used in German brewing since the eleventh century. They are rich in estrogen, so they act as a male anaphrodisiac: excessive consumption of beer can therefore lead to a loss of libido. Hops are highly sedative and calming for the spirit, helping to smooth *Qi* circulation and relax the nervous system, so they are ideal for stress, irritability, and insomnia. They are also a bitter digestive stimulant, useful in poor appetite and sluggish liver function.

CAUTIONS Should not be taken by those suffering from depression; the hormonal content may disrupt the normal menstrual cycle in regular use.

PASSIFLORA INCARNATA Passion-flower

PARTS USED *aerial parts* TASTE *bland* CHARACTER *cold, dry* MERIDIANS *heart, lung, liver* ACTIONS *analgesic, anti-spasmodic, bitter, cooling, hypotensive, sedative, heart tonic, relaxes blood vessels*

USES Passion-flower takes its name from the religious symbolism of its flowers (thought to represent Christ's Crucifixion). It originated in North America, where it was used for swellings and epilepsy. Today it is regarded as an effective but gentle sedative and painkiller, used largely for insomnia and to reduce high blood pressure. It is gentle enough for children and can be used for hyperactivity and restlessness. It also eases tremors in the elderly, including those in Parkinson's disease, and can help to relieve the vertigo of Ménière's disease, which affects the inner ear.

CAUTIONS Avoid in pregnancy; may cause drowsiness.

OTHER HERBS THAT MAY BE HELPFUL
saffron (p.181) ● ashwagandha (p.107) ● shatavari (p.105)
● sandalwood (p.81) ● camphor (p.157) ● vervain (p.87)
● betony (p.121) ● gotu kola (p.106)

VERVAIN

Spiritual problems

*Modern Western society is renowned for its lack
of spirituality—seen not only in falling church
attendance but in our preoccupation with possessions.
Today's separation of spirit from physical well-being is a
reflection of the "mechanistic" approach that started with
René Descartes. Until well into the seventeenth century
illness was believed to be due as much to spiritual transgression as to
invading micro-organisms and a priest/shaman was essential to effect
any cure. Old herbals frequently combine prayers with a list of herbal
remedies, and in earlier ages the healing powers of plants were enhanced
by gathering them at sacred times or by praying to relevant deities.*

*Today many people find it difficult to separate "mind" and "spirit"—a
confusion not helped by the nineteenth-century translators of Sigmund
Freud (1856–1939), who translated the German die Selle (soul) as "mind"
and used the Greek word psyche (soul) to imply mental processes (an
error that has been described as a "cosmic Freudian slip").*

*Neglecting our spiritual needs can damage our health. In both Chinese
and ayurvedic tradition, for example, the heart is closely associated with
spiritual influences—the focus of Shen (spirit) or home of the atman, the
true or divine aspect of our beings. As one ayurvedic specialist puts it:
"Heart disease reflects deeply seated issues of identity, feeling, and
consciousness...[this] is denied in our culture... Many of us literally die
of broken hearts or spiritual starvation."*

GANODERMA LUCIDEM   Reishi mushroom/*Ling Zhi*

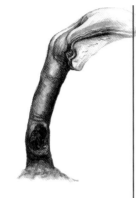

PARTS USED *fruiting body* TASTE *sweet* CHARACTER *slightly warm* MERIDIANS *lung, heart, spleen, liver, kidney* ACTIONS *antiviral, immune stimulant, expectorant, antitussive, antihistaminic, antitumor, hypotensive, reduces cholesterol*

USES The reishi mushroom was highly regarded by Taoists as a spiritual tonic and one that could enhance longevity. It was believed to be especially good for heart *Qi*, to calm *Shen* (spirit), and tonify *Qi* and blood. It is is traditionally used for general debility, lung problems (including asthma and chronic bronchitis), and for problems related to heart disharmonies, such as insomnia, palpitations, forgetfulness, and hypertension. It is now known to stimulate the immune system and has been used for chronic fatigue syndrome/ME and AIDS.
CAUTIONS Avoid if there are no signs of weakness or deficiency.

OCIMUM SPP.   Basil/*tulsi*

PARTS USED *leaves, essential oil* TASTE *pungent, sweet* CHARACTER *heating, dry* MERIDIANS *kidney, lung* ACTIONS *antidepressant, antiseptic, adrenal-cortex stimulant, anti-emetic, tonic, carminative, febrifugal, expectorant*

USES Familiar in Europe as a culinary herb (*O. basilicum*), basil has a close relative, sacred basil (*O. sanctum*), that is regarded in India as a potent tonic—sacred to Vishnu and Krishna and capable of "opening the heart and mind." It bestows love and devotion. It is useful in chills and clears excess *kapha* from the nasal passages and lungs. In the West it is recommended for digestive upsets and to clear intestinal parasites. The oil can be used as a nerve tonic, antidepressant, and digestive remedy or may be added to chest rubs.
CAUTIONS Avoid in high *pitta* conditions; avoid basil oil in pregnancy.

OTHER HERBS THAT MAY BE HELPFUL
rosemary (p.71) ● *sage (p.49)* ● *ginseng (p.106)* ● *gotu kola (p.106)* ● *ashwagandha (p.107)* ● *shatavari (p.105)* ● *He Shou Wu (p.179)* ● *walnut (p.165)* ● *cinnamon (p.129)*

DRIED GINGKO

Old age

In the West the illnesses associated with old age tend to be defined in terms of "wear and tear": degenerative diseases affect ailing organs, and tissues are aged by increasing oxidation as an inevitable consequence of normal living. Treatments tend to focus on antioxidant remedies (as seen in the bewildering array of health-food products), with surgery and replacement joints when the old organs become too worn to "repair." Age is associated with decline—in both health and mental faculties—and is to be deferred with hormone-replacement programs and facelifts for as long as possible. Herbs such as ginkgo, which strengthen cerebral circulation, are increasingly popular in the West in this battle with time.

In Eastern tradition age is venerated, so much of the depression and melancholy of the West are unknown. In Chinese theory aging is seen as inevitable, but is associated with the natural run-down in congenital Jing (vital essence). This can be deferred by a healthy lifestyle boosting acquired Jing, helped by kidney tonics to strengthen essence and combat associated symptoms, including graying hair, impotence, backache, deafness, and menopausal problems.

In ayurveda old age is associated with vata, bringing coldness, dryness, and decay—but as the body weakens, an awareness of what lies beyond it is believed to increase, and old age is associated with wisdom and spirituality.

CODONOPSIS PILOSULA *Dang Shen*

PARTS USED *root* TASTE *sweet* CHARACTER *neutral*
MERIDIANS *spleen, lung* ACTIONS *blood tonic (increases red
blood cells), hypotensive, immune stimulant, nervous stimulant,
hyperglycemic*

USES *Dang Shen* is often used as a rather less
expensive alternative to Korean ginseng *(Ren Shen)*.
The herb is considered to be gentler and more *Yin* in
character and is traditionally taken by nursing mothers.
Gentle it may be, but it is still an effective *Qi* tonic for
the spleen, stomach, middle *Jiao*, and lungs, being
ideal for deficiency ailments characterized by tiredness,
loss of appetite, aching limbs, palpitations, chronic
coughs, and shortness of breath. It also helps body
fluids *(Jin-Ye)*, so it is a good remedy in thirst and
chronic hemorrhage.
CAUTIONS Avoid in cases of attack by "external evils."

COMMIPHORA MUKUL *Guggul/guggula*

PARTS USED *oleo-gum resin* TASTE *bitter, pungent, astringent,
sweet* CHARACTER *heating* MERIDIANS *lung, liver*
ACTIONS *rejuvenative tonic, stimulant, alterative, nervine,
antispasmodic, analgesic, expectorant, astringent, antiseptic*

USES Guggul is a close relative of myrrh, but is
regarded as more important in ayurvedic medicine. It is
believed to be purifying and rejuvenating and forms the
basis of a series of remedial products known as
gugguls. Traditionally it is used for *vata* problems, such
as arthritis, which is common in old age. More recent
research has found that *guggul* also reduces high
blood-cholesterol levels. In addition *guggul* has been
shown to be anti-inflammatory, to stimulate white blood-
cell production, reduce blood clotting, and help protect
heart tissue in degenerative diseases.
CAUTIONS Avoid in pregnancy and breastfeeding.

DIMOCARPUS LONGAN Longan/*Long Yan Rou*

PARTS USED *fruit* TASTE *sweet* CHARACTER *warm*
MERIDIANS *heart, spleen* ACTIONS *nourishing, sedative,
antifungal*

USES Longan fruits are rather like raisins and are
delicious in cooking. They have been used in Chinese
medicine for at least 2,000 years and are believed to
nourish the blood, calm the spirit, and tonify the heart
and spleen. As such they can combat insomnia,
forgetfulness, dizziness, and palpitations, which are
usually dismissed simply as the consequences of aging
in Western medicine. The herb is also a good tonic
following childbirth.

CAUTIONS Avoid in fire and damp phlegm stagnation.

GINKGO BILOBA Ginkgo/*Bai Guo*

PARTS USED *leaves, seeds* TASTE *sweet, bitter, astringent*
CHARACTER *neutral (seeds are slightly toxic)* MERIDIANS *lung,
kidney* Actions: *leaves—vasodilator, circulatory stimulant, anti-
inflammatory; seeds—astringent, antifungal, antibacterial*

USES The seeds *(Bai Guo)* are used in Chinese
medicine to treat asthma and urinary problems and it is
only in the past 15 years or so that ginkgo leaves have
been investigated. The herb inhibits platelet activating
factor (PAF), which causes the blood to become more
sticky, so can help to prevent blood clots. PAF contributes
to the body's allergic response, confirming ginkgo's
traditional use as an anti-asthmatic. Ginkgo has also
been shown to improve cerebral circulation, which has
led many to regard it as an anti-aging remedy, since
poor blood supply to the brain is a cause of apparent
confusion in the elderly.

CAUTIONS High doses of the seeds (in excess of
10g by decoction) can lead to skin disorders and
headaches; the herb is restricted in some countries.

LIGUSTRUM LUCIDUM   Glossy privet/*Nu Zhen Zi*

PARTS USED *berries* TASTE *sweet, bitter* CHARACTER *neutral*
MERIDIANS *liver, kidney* ACTIONS *antibacterial, cardiotonic, diuretic, immune stimulant*

USES *Nu Zhen Zi* is the berry from the glossy privet bush, which is grown in the West as a garden ornamental. The herb has been used in China for at least 2,000 years and is one of the more important remedies for nourishing deficient liver and replenishing kidney *Yin*. It therefore helps to combat some of the signs of aging and has a traditional reputation for restoring the color to prematurely graying hair and improving the eyesight. It is a popular menopausal remedy in China and is also used for lower back pains associated with kidney weakness; as a liver tonic it is also good for strengthening the knees.

CAUTIONS Avoid in diarrhea with "deficient *Yang*."

STACHYS OFFICINALIS   Betony

PARTS USED *aerial parts* TASTE *bitter, astringent*
CHARACTER *cold, dry* MERIDIANS *lung, liver* ACTIONS *sedative, bitter digestive remedy, nervine, circulatory tonic (particularly for cerebral circulation), astringent*

USES Although held in high regard by the Anglo-Saxons, betony has now fallen from fashion. It is an excellent remedy for headaches and nervous upsets, useful for liver and respiratory disorders and makes a pleasant tisane for everyday drinking. The herb is also a uterine stimulant and can be helpful for period pain: it was traditionally used in childbirth for difficult or stalled labor. It smooths *Qi* circulation and its action on the liver helps to calm fiery emotions and nervous irritability. It helps with cerebral circulation, so can be especially useful in old age.

CAUTIONS Avoid in pregnancy, except during labor.

121

Holistic health tips

• Emotional upsets may be closely associated with physical well-being: shallow breathing can increase feelings of anxiety and panic, so practice regular abdominal breathing. Place your hands on the area below the navel, sit on a chair or cross-legged on the floor (whichever is more comfortable) and breathe so that the abdomen rises in inhalation and falls on exhalation. Repeat for 10–15 breaths two or three times a day.

• Simple meditation techniques can help calm the mind and may be performed at any time and anywhere: curl the corners of the mouth into a half-smile, focus on the smile, and breathe deeply four times. Repeat once or twice a day—wherever you happen to be.

• Yoga breathing exercises can also help calm the mind. Start by sitting comfortably with your hands placed palm down on your lower abdomen. Breathe in slowly through your nose while counting up to five and concentrate on how the breath travels through your body and how your abdomen moves gently upward. Hold your breath for a further count of five while concentrating, then breathe out through the mouth while making a "huu" sound, also to the count of five. Continue for 5–10 minutes.

• Qigong breathing can be more dynamic: try "healthy walking." Stand straight, still, and well-balanced with the mind focused on the lower abdomen, then walk forward with your heels touching the ground and your toes lifted high, while relaxing the head and waist and swinging the arms gently from side to side so that one hand comes to rest on the abdomen at the completion of each step. Look to left and to right while walking, as if (as the Chinese say) admiring flowers: "In flowering shrubs you walk leisurely with a smile on your face and light at heart." Breathing should be through the nose— breathing in for two steps and out for one.

CARDIOVASCULAR SYSTEM
Western Approach

Ever since William Harvey (1578–1657) provided the first scientific explanation for the circulation of blood in the seventeenth century, the heart has been seen in Western medicine as little more than a glorified pump, while blood vessels and their behavior are described in terms of fluid mechanics.

Below *Blood-letting was commonly practiced as a part of Galenic medicine.*

One half of the heart pumps blood around the lungs, where it takes in oxygen from the air we breathe. The other half pumps the oxygenated blood around the body, where the oxygen is transferred from red blood cells (which transport it in hemoglobin) to our tissues.

Failure of the system leads to oxygen starvation in the vital organs. This may be because the red blood cells are lacking in hemoglobin (iron-deficient anemia), so the transport mechanism fails; because the heart is weakened and fails to pump efficiently; because the lungs are congested and cannot take in air; because the blood vessels are clogged with fat (arteriosclerosis), rather like a furred-up kettle—or it may occur for many other reasons (all traditionally explained in terms reminiscent of schoolbook physics).

Below *A happy, generous disposition and rosy-cheeked good health are characteristic of a "sanguine" temperament.*

Earlier ages viewed the blood rather differently: to the Galenic physicians it was one of the four humors that affected our health, well-being, and temperament. An excess, as in fever, needed to be removed by "bleeding," that strange processes of drawing 1pt/500ml or more at a time from a vein during illness. The right balance, however, led to the "sanguine" temperament—a happy, generous disposition.

123

CARDIOVASCULAR SYSTEM
Chinese Approach

Above Chuan Xiong, or Szechuan lovage, is used in TCM to invigorate the blood and strengthen Xue.

Below In TCM one branch of the heart acupuncture meridian runs across the chest and then along the midline of the inner arm to the little finger.

In Chinese theory the heart is one of the five solid or Zang organs, while blood is Xue—one of the five fundamental substances that are essential for life.

Despite the limitations of Taoist physiology, early Chinese physicians did link the heart with the blood: it was said to control the circulation and blood vessels and was regarded as the ruling member of the Zang-Fu organs, controlling all life processes. The heart was also closely associated with the soul and emotions: it is the seat of Shen, or spirit, and is seen to control "mental activities." Erratic or manic behaviour is thus seen as a heart disorder—and many Chinese "heart" herbs "calm the spirit" and are, in Western terms, effective sedatives for the nervous system.

Blood is, therefore, rather more than simply a means of transporting nutrients to the tissues. Xue is formed from a mixture of nourishing Qi, food essence, and body fluids (Jin-Ye), so it is Yin in character. Like the heart, it is linked to mental activities: both Xue and Qi encourage clear thinking and vigor.

In the Zang-Fu model, the liver is said to "store blood," so any damage to the liver is likely to harm blood, with weak liver Qi being one of the most common causes of "blood stagnation" or stasis; this is one of the most significant causes of internal illness in TCM. Blood stasis is seen as some sort of blockage in the normal circulation—but that does not always mean our Western concept of a blood clot. In addition to Qi stagnation or deficiency, blood stasis can be caused by cold entering Xue, causing it to congeal and slow down; by heat increasing the flow and leading to hemorrhage; or by injuries or wounds.

As in Chinese theory, ayurveda places the soul—the *atman* or divine self—in the heart. Heart disease is therefore often seen as linked to some deep-seated emotional or spiritual issue. These factors are always considered first by ayurvedic practitioners, rather than concentrating initially on poor diet or physical aspects of the problem.

The heart *chakra* (energy center), or *anahata*, is the fourth of the seven *chakras* that run from the base of the spine to the crown of the head, and it is associated with the color yellow. This *chakra* is believed by some to be strengthened and supported by the emotion of love.

Above *The heart chakra is one of the seven energy centers lying on an imaginary line down the center of the body.*

As always, ayurveda regards problems of the heart in terms of imbalance in the three humors. *Pitta* is closely associated with the blood, so heart disease is often a *pitta* problem: a red-faced, ambitious, bad-tempered executive who has a sudden heart attack in midlife is the archetypal excess-*pitta* individual. *Vata* imbalance is more likely to occur in old age when this humor dominates, so the problems of old age—hardening of the arteries and weakened heart muscles—are seen as a drying of the tissues associated with excess *vata*. *Kapha* is associated with phlegm, damp, and obesity—another obvious explanation for a third category of heart and vascular disorders.

Right *Yarrow flowers are used in ayurveda to reduce excess pitta and so may be useful in heart disease.*

125

OTHER HERBS THAT MAY BE HELPFUL
turmeric (p.130) ● Dang Gui (p.173) ● amalaki (p.64)
● Shu Di Huang (p.53) ● Chi Shao Yao (p.68) ● ginger (p.185)

TURMERIC

Blood and circulatory disorders

Circulatory problems such as arteriosclerosis, or hardening of the arteries, are often explained in Western terms as a "furring-up of the pipes"— excess cholesterol in the blood, leading to fatty deposits in the blood vessels, which eventually cause narrowing and disease. Orthodox doctors once preached a universal message of low-cholesterol diets to combat the problem, although this has become less fashionable in recent years with the realization that the body will produce its own extra cholesterol if nutritional supplies are limited; cholesterol may, in fact, be a valuable lubricant to keep the blood vessels smooth and the blood flowing freely.

As well as diet, Western practitioners generally blame smoking, excess alcohol, diabetes, thyroid problems, and chronic high blood pressure for arteriosclerosis. Using fish-oil supplements, additional vitamin E or C, and eating plenty of garlic are commonly suggested treatments.

ASHTRAY

Arteriosclerosis is in turn blamed for many heart disorders, as well as being a common cause of strokes if the arteries in the brain are affected. Problems with cerebral circulation associated with hardening arteries can cause confusion in the elderly and may be mistaken for dementia.

In ayurveda arteriosclerosis may be due to kapha-style fat accumulation or to excess vata occurring in old age. Aloe-vera gel combined with turmeric or safflower is often used in ayurvedic treatment, and there is also an emphasis on low-kapha diets—cutting down on foods that encourage the formation of phlegm and mucus and concentrating instead on fruit and vegetables, rather than avoiding all fats and simply cutting them out of the diet.

The Chinese are more likely to blame circulatory problems on blood stasis, due to cold or heat affecting the blood or some sort of Qi weakness. Herbs that are specifics for "moving blood" or stimulating liver or heart Qi to help the circulation are used in such cases. This category of herbs again includes turmeric and safflower, which are used where blood stasis may be involved in causing swellings or pain.

ORANGE

Poor circulation—seen in cold fingers and toes—may be a harmless congenital problem or may suggest heart weakness. Herbalists also associate poor circulation with chronic skin or arthritic conditions and use a variety of stimulants, such as tabasco pepper, to encourage blood flow. In symbolic Chinese tradition cinnamon twigs (Gui Zhi) are believed to send blood to our extremities (as the twigs are found on the extremes of the trees), while cinnamon bark (Rou Gui, which is wrapped around the body of the tree) is believed to be more warming for the trunk and central areas.

Heat in the blood is seen as a cause of hemorrhage in both ayurveda and Chinese theory and can also contribute to inflammatory disorders and skin problems, such as eczema. Herbs like Chi Shao Yao are described as being cooling to the blood and are used in treating both bleeding disorders and fevers.

ALLIUM SATIVUM Garlic/*Da Suan/rashona*

PARTS USED *bulb, oil* TASTE *pungent* CHARACTER *warm*
MERIDIANS *spleen, stomach, lung, large intestine*
ACTIONS *antiparasitic, antibiotic, expectorant, diaphoretic, hypotensive, antithrombotic, reduces cholesterol levels, hypoglycemic, antihistaminic*

USES Garlic has been used for treating colds and catarrh since ancient Egyptian times. Modern research has also confirmed its role as an anti-cholesterol remedy in treating heart and circulatory problems. The Chinese view it as an antiparasitic remedy for treating hookworms and pinworms. In ayurveda it is seen as a rejuvenating tonic, especially for bone and nerve tissue, and it will also cleanse *ama* and excess *kapha*. It is *tamasic* in character and excess can dull the mind.
CAUTIONS Can irritate weak stomachs and sensitive skins; avoid high doses during pregnancy and when breastfeeding.

CAPSICUM FRUTESCENS Tabasco pepper/*marishi-phalum*

PART USED *fruit* TASTE *pungent* CHARACTER *hot*
MERIDIANS *lung, spleen* ACTIONS *circulatory stimulant, tonic, antispasmodic, diaphoretic, gastric stimulant, carminative, antiseptic, antibacterial, analgesic; use topically as a counterirritant and rubefacient*

USES A spicy flavoring, tabasco pepper has been used in Europe since the sixteenth century to improve the circulation and combat chills. It is a *Yang* remedy, clearing cold and balancing *Yin* excess. Recent studies suggest that it can be used externally to relieve the pain of shingles. In ayurveda it is regarded as food for *agni* (digestive fire), although it is termed *rajasic*, so an excess can lead to mental disturbance.
CAUTIONS Avoid in stomach ulceration, pregnancy, and breastfeeding; do not eat the seeds on their own; avoid touching the eyes or cuts after handling fresh peppers.

CARTHAMUS TINCTORIUS Safflower/*Hong Hua*

PARTS USED *flower* TASTE *pungent* CHARACTER *warm*
MERIDIANS *liver, heart* ACTIONS *circulatory stimulant, anti-inflammatory, febrifugal, analgesic, reduces cholesterol levels*

USES Safflower is said in Chinese tradition to "move the blood," so it is used for painful swellings and other problems related to blood stasis, including period pain. The flowers are also used externally in poultices for wounds and sores and are taken in infusions for fevers and shin rashes associated with excess heat. Studies have suggested that the herb can also lower cholesterol levels and may stimulate the immune system. The seed oil also helps to regulate excess cholesterol and is rich in essential fatty acids, so it makes a valuable supplement in chronic skin and arthritic problems.
CAUTIONS Avoid using the flowers in pregnancy (the seed oil used in cooking is quite safe).

CINNAMOMUM CASSIA Cinnamon/*Gui Zhi*/*twak*

PARTS USED *twigs* TASTE *pungent, sweet* CHARACTER *warm*
MERIDIANS *heart, lung, urinary bladder* ACTIONS *antibacterial, antifungal, antiviral, analgesic, carminative, cardiotonic, diuretic*

USES *Gui Zhi* is a useful remedy for "exterior cold"—as in common colds and arthritic problems associated with cold. It also strengthens heart *Yang*, so it is used for palpitations and shortness of breath and is combined with *Fu Ling, Gan Cao,* or *Dan Shen* for various heart-related problems, including angina pectoris. It is believed to warm the channels and collaterals, improving the circulation of *Yang Qi*. In ayurveda it is seen as *sattvic*, strengthening the circulation and heart, and it also encourages *agni*.
CAUTIONS Avoid in feverish conditions, excess heat or fire syndromes, and in pregnancy.

129

CURCUMA LONGA Turmeric/*Jiang Huang/haridra*

PARTS USED *rhizome* TASTE *pungent, bitter* CHARACTER *warm* MERIDIANS *liver, spleen* ACTIONS *stimulant, carminative, alterative, wound healer, antibacterial, anti-inflammatory, reduces cholesterol levels, stimulates bile production*

USES Turmeric is one of the more familiar Indian spices. It helps to normalize gut flora and stimulate digestion and is also used in ayurveda for cleansing the *chakras* and purifying the blood. Externally it was used with honey for sprains and bruises, or taken as a milk decoction to cleanse and improve the skin and reduce inflammation in arthritis. It is also believed to help stretch the ligaments, so it is popular with those practicing *hatha yoga*. The Chinese name means "yellow ginger" and the herb is used to regulate *Qi*, resolve blood stagnation, and clear pain—especially in traumatic injuries and period pain.

CAUTIONS Can cause skin rashes in sensitive individuals and may increase photosensitivity.

FAGOPYRUM ESCULENTUM Buckwheat

PARTS USED *flowers and leaves* TASTE *sweet* CHARACTER *warm* MERIDIANS *liver, stomach, spleen* ACTIONS *vein tonic and restorative, hypotensive, peripheral vasodilator, anticoagulant*

USES Buckwheat was brought to Europe by the Crusaders as a cereal crop and is still used for making crêpes in Brittany and blini in Russia. It is rich in rutin, which strengthens the blood vessels and controls bleeding, so it can be helpful in a range of circulatory disorders, including spontaneous bleeding and capillary fragility. It is useful in high blood pressure and can ease chilblains and frostbite. The herb is also a good source of magnesium and has been used to protect the body from damage in radiation treatment.

CAUTIONS None noted.

PRUNUS PERSICA Peach/*Tao Ren*

PARTS USED *seeds* TASTE *sweet, bitter* CHARACTER *neutral*
MERIDIANS *lung, liver, large intestine* ACTIONS *antitussive,
antiasthmatic, astringent, antibacterial, analgesic, diuretic,
and anti-inflammatory*

USES In Chinese medicine peach seeds are believed
to invigorate the blood and circulation, and are used
as a mild laxative and as a cough remedy. They are
included in many remedies for menstrual problems and
in invigorating remedies for constipation due to old age
or debility. They are combined with *Dang Gui* to
stimulate the blood and circulation or with rhubarb root,
licorice, cinnamon twigs *(Gui Zhi)*, and *Dang Gui* for
menstrual problems associated with blood stagnation.
CAUTIONS The seeds/stones from all *Prunus* spp. are
potentially toxic and may cause drowsiness due to
traces of cynaogenic compounds.

ZIZIPHUS JUJUBA Chinese-date/*Da Zao*

PARTS USED *fruit* TASTE *sweet* CHARACTER *warm*
MERIDIANS *spleen, stomach.* ACTIONS *nutrient, protective
against liver damage*

USES *Da Zao* literally means "big date" and the fruits
are one of the important "harmonizers" of Chinese
medicine, often added to prescriptions to help modify
any conflicts in the action of the different ingredients.
They are also used to tonify spleen and stomach *Qi*,
strengthen "nourishing *Qi*" *(Ying Qi)* and blood, and
calm the spirit *(Shen)*. From three to ten dates are usually
added to a daily decoction *(Tang)*. The dates are often
used for general debility and lack of appetite, and in
anemia for palpitations and irritability associated with
"deficient heart energy" or "constrained liver *Qi*."
CAUTIONS Avoid in cases of excess dampness, food
stagnation, or phlegm syndromes.

OTHER HERBS THAT MAY BE HELPFUL
hawthorn (p.137) ● *vervain (p.87)* ● *Ju Hua (p.64)*
● *cinnamon (p.129))* ● *garlic (p.128)*

MOTHERWORT

Heart disorders

Heart disease is one of the commonest

causes of death in Western society, with its

prevalence being variously blamed on poor diet,

stress, or pollution. In Eastern theory, however, the

heart is synonymous with the spirit or soul and some alternative-health

practitioners view the lack of spirituality in our society as a contributory

factor in today's high incidence of heart disease.

In Western terms heart disease may be linked to arteriosclerosis

(see p.126), with the narrowing of the coronary arteries often leading to

"heart attacks," as tissues are starved of oxygen, and to problems with

heart valves. Angina pectoris, which is typified by a severe pain in the

chest or shoulders that is relieved by rest, is also linked to this sort of

coronary disease. It can also be exacerbated by

emotional upsets and stress.

The Chinese define angina and heart attacks in

terms of blockage in the heart channel due to

blood stasis or phlegm. Differential diagnosis is

obviously important—if blood stasis is to blame,

then treatment will focus on smoothing the

flow of Qi and blood, using herbs such as Dan

GARLIC

Shen, safflower, and Chi Shao Yao; while too

much phlegm will be resolved by using aromatic herbs and tonics to

regulate spleen function—remedies such as Chen Pi and Bai Zhu.

ACHILLEA MILLEFOLIUM   Yarrow/*I Chi Kao/gandana*

PARTS USED *leaves, flowers, essential oil* TASTE *bitter, astringent* CHARACTER *cool, dry* MERIDIANS *spleen, liver, urinary bladder, kidney* ACTIONS *aerial parts/flowers— astringent, diaphoretic, peripheral vasodilator, digestive stimulant, restorative for menstrual system, febrifugal; essential oil—anti-inflammatory, anti-allergenic, antispasmodic*

USES A common meadow herb, yarrow is a traditional wound healer and is also taken for colds, hay fever, and catarrh. As a diuretic, it can be used for urinary problems and to counter fluid retention or reduce blood pressure. It is used to combat excess *pitta* in ayurveda and to normalize bile and ease inflammations in the digestive tract. It helps to clear *Qi* stagnation and combat liver *Qi* constraint and deficiency.

CAUTIONS Avoid in pregnancy as it is a uterine stimulant; the fresh plant may cause contact dermatitis and, rarely, may increase the skin's photosensitivity.

ALPINIA SPP.   Galangal/*Gao Liang Jiang/kulanjian*

TASTE *pungent* CHARACTER *hot, dry* MERIDIANS *spleen, stomach* ACTIONS *carminative, digestive tonic, promotes sweating, prevents vomiting, stimulant, antifungal*

USES Galangal *(A. galanga)* was brought to Europe by Arab traders and was a favorite of the abbess and healer Hildegard of Bingen (1098–1179), who used it for a wide range of heart disorders, including angina pectoris. Studies by modern German followers of Hildegard suggest that drops of galangal tincture can be used, much as nitroglycerine, to avert angina attacks. Traditionally the herb is used as a warming, digestive remedy and for travel sickness and is very similar to ginger. Lesser galangal *(A. officinarum)* is used in similar ways as a digestive remedy in India and is known as *Gao Liang Jiang* in China.

CAUTIONS Avoid in "deficient *Yin*" with heat symptoms.

LEONURUS SPP. Motherwort/*Yi Mu Cao*

PARTS USED *aerial parts* **TASTE** *pungent* **CHARACTER** *cool*
MERIDIANS *heart, liver, kidney* **ACTIONS** *uterine stimulant, relaxant, cardiac tonic, carminative*

USES Motherwort (*L. cardiaca*) is generally used as a heart tonic and sedative, although it takes its name from its traditional use to calm anxiety in childbirth. Recent research suggests that it can help prevent thrombosis, and it is popular for treating menopausal upsets and premenstrual syndrome. It helps to circulate *Qi* and relieve heart *Qi* constraint, as well as blood stagnation contributing to menstrual problems. It is used for angina pectoris and is often combined with vervain as a relaxing nervine in menopausal upsets and other emotional problems. The Chinese use a related species (*L. heterophylus*) as a circulatory stimulant and to relieve menstrual problems.

CAUTIONS Avoid in pregnancy, except during labor, as it is a uterine stimulant.

OPHIOPOGON JAPONICUS *Mai Men Dong*

TASTE *sweet, slightly bitter* **CHARACTER** *cool* **MERIDIANS** *heart, lung, stomach* **ACTIONS** *tonic, sedative, antitussive, hypoglycemic, antibacterial*

USES *Mai Men Dong* is one of the major herbs for strengthening *Yin* energies; it also clears heat and encourages body fluids (*Jin-Ye*). It is nourishing for the stomach and heart and helps to soothe the lung, so is ideal for dry coughs or where there is thick sputum that is difficult to expectorate, sore throats, and constipation. Its calming action on the heart and spirit (*Shen*) makes it ideal for palpitations, insomnia, and anxiety that may be associated with what would be described in the West as "nervous tension."

CAUTIONS Avoid in "deficient spleen" and loose stool.

SALVIA MILTIORRHIZA Chinese sage/*Dan Shen*

PARTS USED *root, rhizome* TASTE *bitter* CHARACTER *slightly cold* MERIDIANS *heart, liver, pericardium* ACTIONS *anticoagulant, antibacterial, immune stimulant, circulatory stimulant, peripheral vasodilator, promotes tissue repair, sedative, reduces cholesterol levels, hypoglycemic*

USES Chinese sage is an important heart and blood remedy, which has been shown in clinical trials to help both heart disease and problems with cerebral circulation. It is used for angina pectoris and is said to "invigorate the blood circulation" and clear blood stagnation, clear heat, and "calm the spirit," thus soothing irritability. As it affects the liver meridian, *Dan Shen* is also used for period pains and irregular or scanty menstruation.

CAUTIONS Use with care if there is no blood stagnation.

ZIZIPHUS JUJUBA VAR. SPINOSA   Wild date seeds/*Suan Zao Ren*

PARTS USED *seeds* TASTE *sweet, sour* CHARACTER *neutral* MERIDIANS *liver, heart* ACTIONS *sedative, analgesic, reduces body temperature, hypotensive*

USES A calming herb for irritability, palpitations, and insomnia, wild date seeds are also nourishing for the heart and liver and helpful for "deficient heart blood and *Yin*," a syndrome often typified by these symptoms, as well as for deficient liver blood and excess heat in the liver, when it is often used with *Fu Ling* and other herbs. *Suan Zao Ren* also prevents abnormal sweating (including night sweats), so can help ease menopausal symptoms. Modern research has shown that it can reduce high blood pressure and calm heart action.

CAUTIONS Avoid if there are excess heat syndromes and acute infections.

OTHER HERBS THAT MAY BE HELPFUL
Ju Hua (p.64) ● *garlic (p.128)* ● *Dan Shen (p.135)*
● *turmeric (p.130)* ● *motherwort (p.134)* ● *galangal (p.133)*
● *buckwheat (p.130)*

BUCKWHEAT

Blood-pressure problems

Until the arrival of the sphygmomanometer a century or so ago, blood

pressure was an unknown quantity. Today, coin-in-the-slot "read your BP"

machines and kits for home use abound, and avoiding hypertension

(raised blood pressure) has become an obsession for many. The

sphygmomanometer records the pressure when the heart contracts

(systolic) and when it relaxes (diastolic). Everyone is different and some

people have naturally occurring—and quite safe—blood-pressure readings

that are higher or lower than average.

Traditional therapies simply treat raised blood pressure as a heart

disorder, for symptoms can be very similar: Ju Hua, for example, lowers

blood pressure, but this would be seen as a problem relating to another

syndrome, such as ascending liver Yang, rather than as a disease in itself.

Low blood pressure is likewise a symptom and may be associated with

blood loss, general debility, anemia, or shock. Readings below 110/65

are usually classified as low, although some people have naturally low

BLOOD-PRESSURE READINGS

The typical readings for a young, healthy person are 120/80; the average for the over-60s is likely to be 165/85. If the lower reading (diastolic) is above 90 or below 65, then professional investigation may well be necessary.

blood pressure and are none the worse for it: in fact, they generally live longer than average. If it is a problem, symptoms are likely to include dizziness, headaches, fainting, anxiety, and panic attacks: herbalists generally treat these symptoms with circulatory stimulants and tonic herbs.

CRATAEGUS SPP. Hawthorn/*Shan Zha*

PARTS USED *flowering tops, berries* TASTE *sour, sweet*
CHARACTER *slightly warm* MERIDIANS *spleen, stomach, liver*
ACTIONS *regulates blood pressure, peripheral vasodilator,
cardiac tonic, reduces cholesterol levels, relaxant,
antispasmodic, diuretic, antibacterial*

USES European species of hawthorn (*C. laevigata* and
C. monogyna) are widely used as a cardiac tonic to
improve peripheral circulation, regulate heart rate and
blood pressure, and improve coronary blood flow. As
an astringent it was more often used in the past for sore
throats and diarrhea. In contrast, the closely related
Chinese species (*C. pinnatifida*) is seen as a digestive
remedy as well as a circulatory stimulant. It is used for
digestive problems such as indigestion, abdominal
bloating discomfort, and diarrhea, as well as for
menstrual problems and coronary heart disorders.
CAUTIONS Use cautiously in "deficient spleen and
stomach" or if there is acid regurgitation.

SCUTELLARIA BAICALENSIS Baikal skullcap/*Huang Qin*

PARTS USED *root* TASTE *bitter* CHARACTER *cold*
MERIDIANS *lung, heart, stomach, gall bladder, large
intestine* ACTIONS *antibacterial, antispasmodic, diuretic,
febrifugal, reduces cholesterol levels, hypotensive, increases
bile flow, sedative*

USES Chinese skullcap is primarily used for clearing
damp-heat. It also eliminates heat in the lungs, calms
liver *Yang*, and will "calm the fetus" in threatened
miscarriage. It is used with other cooling herbs for
feverish chills. Internal "damp-heat" problems generally
manifest as dysentery-like disorders and the herb is use
for gastroenteritis, diarrhea, and urinary-tract infections.
It is also used for high blood pressure, for "heat in the
blood" syndromes, and to stop bleeding.
CAUTIONS Avoid if true heat/dampness symptoms exist.

OTHER HERBS THAT MAY BE HELPFUL
turmeric (p.130) ● *buckwheat (p.130)* ● *witch-hazel (p.155)*

HORSE-CHESTNUT

Venous problems

Veins, unlike arteries, have to help force blood back to the heart, rather than depend on the impetus of the heart's powerful action. The muscles surrounding deep veins can help considerably in this, but the superficial veins in the legs often have little support for forcing blood back to the central pumping system and can become distended and tortuous. These varicosed veins are usually visible as knotted veins on the surface of the legs. They may ache or the surrounding area may swell and feel hot.

Orthodox treatment usually involves surgery to strip and pull the veins back into shape, while a simple preventative is to hose the legs alternately several times with a hot and cold shower, for one or two minutes each morning, to help tonify the muscle action. Putting bricks under the end of the bed to aid venous return at night can also help.

Western herbalists use a variety of venous tonics, such as horse-chestnut and melilot, to ease symptoms of varicose veins; regular exercise and an active lifestyle are among the best preventatives, so it is hardly surprising that traditional Eastern therapies pay scant attention to the problem—it would be seen as an aspect of blood stasis in Chinese theory.

Both ayurveda and Chinese medicine do, however, offer plenty of herbal treatment for hemorrhoids (piles), which are also varicosed veins, but at the end of the lower bowel. Ayurveda views these as vata or pitta problems often related to inadequate agni—turmeric, applied externally as a paste, is a remedy to encourage digestion and tonify the tissues.

AESCULUS HIPPOCASTANUM Horse-chestnut

PARTS USED *seeds, bark* **TASTE** *bitter, pungent*
CHARACTER *cool, dry* **MERIDIANS** *liver* **ACTIONS** *anti-inflammatory, astringent, febrifugal, vasodilator*

USES Horse-chestnut seeds are used for all sorts of venous problems associated with blood stagnation, including varicose veins, hemorrhoids, thrombosis, and skin rashes. They are also used for swollen ankles, chilblains, and night cramps, which can all be associated with blood stagnation; and for menstrual problems associated with blood stasis. The bark is more astringent than the seeds and is occasionally used to relieve the discomfort of diarrhea; it may also be added to remedies for watery catarrh and coughs. The herb is often used in external ointments for both piles and varicose veins, or it may be taken internally.
CAUTIONS None noted.

MELILOTUS OFFICINALE Melilot

PARTS USED *aerial parts* **TASTE** *bitter, pungent*
CHARACTER *cool, dry* **MERIDIANS** *liver, heart, small intestine*
ACTIONS *anticoagulant, antithrombotic, antispasmodic, anti-inflammatory, diuretic, expectorant, sedative, styptic, mild analgesic*

USES Melilot smells of new-mown hay, due to chemicals called coumarins that it contains and which account for much of its antithrombotic action. It is useful for easing the pain of eczema associated with varicose veins and blood stagnation, and can also be helpful for facial neuralgia and rheumatic pains, or applied in eyebaths for conjunctivitis. It is cleansing and useful for pain and inflammation associated with gastroenteritis and colitis; it can also help ease period pain and heavy menstrual bleeding associated with congestion.
CAUTIONS Avoid if using anticoagulant drugs, such as warfarin.

OTHER HERBS THAT MAY BE HELPFUL
ashwagandha (p.107) ● rosemary (p.71) ● betony (p.121)
● Ju Hua (p.64) ● valerian (p.103) ● blue skullcap (p.103)

CHEESE

Migraine

Migraine is associated with constriction of the blood vessels of the brain, followed by expansion and engorgement, with resulting severe headaches, nausea, photosensitivity, emotional stress, and speech difficulties. It is typically preceded by visual disturbances: jagged lights to the edge of the visual field or a sense that there is a strange out-of-focus area in what you see. Occasionally the attack may simply consist of these visual upsets with no subsequent headache. Often only one side of the body is affected: the pain is usually one-sided and there may be pins and needles in one arm or hand as well. Migraines can be associated with gastric disturbance, and frequent bilious attacks in a child may lead to migraine in adulthood.

Rather than just relieve the symptoms, Western herbalists stress the need to identify the underlying cause: this is commonly food intolerance (see box) or may be stress-related.

Traditional therapies rarely separate migraine from other types of headache: ayurveda defines all types in terms of pitta, kapha, or vata imbalance and sees migraines as simply the pitta-vata variety: digestive stimulants may be used as well as tonic herbs— ashwagandha is often used to relieve the exhaustion and stress that contribute to it; nutritive tonics (such as the medicated jelly chyavan prash) are also used.

FOOD INTOLERANCE
Migraine is often the result of food intolerance. Among the more common culprits are red wine, chocolate, pork, citrus fruit, coffee, wheat (gluten), and cheese.

LAVANDULA ANGUSTIFOLIA Lavender

PARTS USED *flowers, essential oil* TASTE *bitter, pungent*
CHARACTER *cool, dry* MERIDIANS *heart, pericardium, liver,
lung* ACTIONS *antiseptic, antibacterial, antidepressant,
carminative, relaxant, anti-spasmodic, circulatory stimulant,
tonic for the nervous system, analgesic, stimulates bile flow*

USES Lavender has been used since Roman times as a
cleansing, aromatic herb. It is helpful for digestive
upsets and is uplifting and antidepressant, so it makes
a valuable addition to remedies for tension and
emotional upsets. It is ideal for migraines and
headaches, both taken internally as a tea made from
the flowers or used as an oil to massage the neck and
temples. Added to bathwater, lavender oil is relaxing
and soothing for nervous tension and insomnia; in
massage oils it can be helpful for muscular aches and
pains, strains, and some rheumatic problems.
CAUTIONS None noted.

TANACETUM PARTHENIUM Feverfew

PARTS USED *aerial parts* TASTE *bitter, pungent*
CHARACTER *cool, dry* MERIDIANS *spleen, liver, kidney, urinary
bladder* ACTIONS *anti-inflammatory, vasodilator, relaxant,
digestive stimulant, anthelmintic, stimulates menstruation*

USES Feverfew is one of the most popular herbs for
treating migraine. The plant has been extensively
researched since the 1970s and its effectiveness
demonstrated in clinical trials. It is also a popular
remedy for arthritis and rheumatism, although many
herbs are more effective. It is a stimulating remedy for
liver *Qi* stagnation and is also anticatarrhal for cold-
damp problems. As an antispasmodic, it can be helpful
for period pain, and it cools minor fevers.
CAUTIONS Avoid if using blood-thinning drugs, such as
warfarin; stop taking it if side effects (usually mouth
ulceration) occur.

Holistic health tips

• Low-cholesterol diets have long been recommended in the West for heart problems, although later research suggests that this is an oversimplification. For those who are suffering from congenital high-cholesterol problems, herbal dietary supplements can help— use plenty of garlic, drink linden teas, and add purslane (Portulaca oleracea) to salads and omelets. All three herbs help to reduce cholesterol levels and combat the risk of arteriosclerosis.

• In ayurvedic theory, water purified by storing it overnight in a copper vessel is believed to prevent arteriosclerosis.

• Heart and high blood-pressure problems are often associated with stress and tension. Combat these with relaxation and meditational techniques: 10 minutes of deep abdominal breathing each day, yoga exercises, Qigong, or t'ai-chi.

• In ayurveda, gems and metals are often worn, or swallowed with water in a specially prepared ash form, for heart problems. Red stones (ruby or garnet) and gold act as heart stimulants, while pearls, green stones (emerald or jade) and silver are calming and relaxing for the heart. Yellow stones (such as topaz) help to tonify heart energies.

• Anger is another contributory factor in heart disease: in Chinese theory this is linked to excess or rising liver fire; in ayurveda with excess pitta; and in the West with short-tempered personality traits. Use cooling remedies, soothing liver herbs—and stay calm.

MUSCLES, BONES, & JOINTS
Western Approach

Above *Burdock is one of the most popular cleansing liver herbs, along with curly dock.*

Below *There are several herbal remedies for the shock and pain of injuries to joints and muscles.*

Rest and anti-inflammatories are the usual orthodox approach to muscular aches and pains, sprains, or inflammatory disorders, such as arthritis and fibrositis. Treatment works through a range of increasingly potent anti-inflammatories, until the patient is faced with a course of steroids or surgery to relieve the pain.

Western herbal medicine regards many musculoskeletal problems as related to digestive weakness and a build-up of toxins. Uric acid salts (urates) are the obvious example, with chemicals building up in the bloodstream, due to poor excretion; they are then deposited in joints, resulting in painful arthritic swellings and gout. Many other toxins produced as by-products from nutrition, or as pollutants in our food, find their way into the system.

The liver is the first line of defense when it comes to absorbing the nutrients from the foods that we eat, so herbalists will often treat chronic muscular or joint problems with cleansing liver herbs to restore normal function and help clear the build-up of toxins. Treatment also includes circulatory stimulants and diuretics to help invigorate the system and clear toxic compounds. In the past sweat-houses, hot baths, and diaphoretics were used to remove as many toxins as possible by all excretion routes.

Herbs that encourage blood flow to the skin (rubefacients) are often applied externally in poultices: in the past the aim would have been to encourage blistering (seen as the visible removal of the toxins).

MUSCLES, BONES, & JOINTS
Chinese Approach

In TCM the various components of the musculoskeletal system are associated with specific elements and, thus, with particular *Zang* organs. Muscles are linked with earth and the spleen; bones with water and the kidneys; and tendons with wood and liver. Disorders in these tissues are therefore taken to imply an underlying weakness or imbalance in the *Zang-Fu* organs.

As with traditional Western theories, muscle pains are thus linked to poor digestion and a failure of the spleen to clear unwanted "turbid" fluids *(Ye)*. The connection between tendons and the liver is often apparent in chronic knee disorders: the knee has more tendons than other parts of the body, and aching knees in the morning after an evening of excess alcohol and rich foods—putting extra strain on the liver—are very common.

As well as being due to these internal factors and imbalances, muscular aches and pains are also attributed to attack by "external evils"—rather like common colds. Wind is one of the main culprits and traditional Chinese theory sees a shifting pattern of twinges, aches, and pains as being typical of the variable nature of wind. Cold and damp are other common causes—again, this is something that even sophisticated twenty-first-century Westerners can appreciate, with arthritic and rheumatic pains often being at their worst when the weather is wet or particularly cold.

Many of the herbs used for aches and pains—such as *Du Huo* and *Gui Zhi*—are the same as those used for common colds associated with "external evils."

Above *Rheumatic and arthritic pains are often worse in cold, damp weather and can be treated with warming, drying remedies.*

MUSCLES, BONES, & JOINTS
Ayurvedic Approach

Above *Massage with medicated oils can help to ease the joints and disperse toxins.*

Below *Dancers and athletes regularly use mahanarayan oil in order to improve joint flexibility.*

Ayurvedic theory views the body as being made up of seven *dhatus*, or tissues. Tissues are linked to particular humors—most (skin, muscle, fat, marrow, and semen) are associated with *kapha*, but blood *(rakta)* is a *pitta* tissue and bones *(asthi)* are associated with *vata*.

Humoral imbalance or particular humor-related disorders are therefore likely to affect the associated tissues. However, any humor can affect any tissue, so although particular tissue problems are more likely when particular humors are in excess—as with bone disorders in old age when *vata* dominates—they can also be affected by imbalances elsewhere. As in traditional Western medicine, ayurveda links muscle *(mamsa)* and bone disorders with toxins building up in the system because of poor *agni* (digestive fire). Treatment will always involve a suitable dietary regime to correct the humoral imbalance, as well as herbs to stimulate *agni* and clear toxins.

As with Chinese theory, muscular aches and pains can develop from both internal (usually excess *ama*—toxic) or external causes. External problems can similarly be linked to the weather, and the *vata*-type arthritis of old age is often more prevalent in windy, damp, or stormy conditions.

Medicated oils are often used in ayurveda to loosen stiff joints and clear toxins. *Mahanarayan* oil, in which the main ingredient is *shatavari*, is one of the more popular. *Narayan* oil (based on *ashwagandha*) is also used for muscle pains and is thought to improve circulation.

OTHER HERBS THAT MAY BE HELPFUL
turmeric (p.130) ● *rosemary (p.71)* ● *St.-John's-wort (p.111)*
● *camomile (p.192)* ● *aloe vera (p.63)*

COMFREY

Traumatic injuries

Traumatic injuries need immediate first aid, as well as calming, sedative remedies to help combat shock and anxiety. Although crude herbs are nowhere near as strong as patent analgesics for easing pain, they can be effective in other ways to promote healing and cell growth. Comfrey, for example, contains a chemical called allantoin, which has been shown to stimulate and speed up cell repair—hence the plant's old country name of "knitbone." Arnica increases the absorption rate from internal bleeding, so it too stimulates repair, especially in bruises that are caused by blood escaping from damaged underlying blood vessels following injury.

ARNICA MONTANA Arnica

PARTS USED *flowers, rhizome* TASTE *sweet, bitter, astringent*
CHARACTER *neutral* MERIDIANS *heart, pericardium*
ACTIONS *anti-inflammatory, healing, circulatory stimulant*

USES Arnica encourages tissue repair after injury, so it is ideal both for accidental damage and for use after surgery; arnica ointments are extremely helpful for sprains and bruises. Internally the herb acts as a circulatory stimulant and is still used as a heart remedy in many parts of Europe—especially in general weakness, palpitations with anxiety, and coronary heart disease. In the past it was given for fevers, general debility, and depression associated with chronic illness.
CAUTIONS The herb is extremely toxic—only take internally in homeopathic doses, unless under professional guidance; do not use on open wounds; may occasionally cause contact dermatitis.

CORYDALIS SOLIDA *Yan Hu Suo*

PARTS USED *rhizome* TASTE *pungent, bitter* CHARACTER *warm* MERIDIANS *liver, spleen* ACTIONS *analgesic, sedative, antispasmodic, adrenal stimulant*

USES *Yan Hu Suo* is one of the most potent painkillers used in Chinese medicine. It is traditionally described as invigorating the circulation to clear blood stasis (believed in TCM to cause pain), and it regulates the circulation of *Qi*. It is used for a wide range of painful conditions, including period pains, lumbago, abdominal pains, and traumatic injuries. Around 2g of powder twice a day is enough to ease even very severe pain. The plant contains the strongly analgesic alkaloid corydaline; the crude powdered root is estimated to be about 1 percent as strong as morphine (enough to make it an extremely effective painkiller). CAUTIONS Avoid in pregnancy.

SYMPHYTUM OFFICINALE Comfrey

PARTS USED *root, leaves* TASTE *sweet, bland, astringent* CHARACTER *cool, moist* MERIDIANS *lung, stomach, bladder* ACTIONS *cell proliferator, astringent, demulcent, wound healer, expectorant*

USES Comfrey has undergone a checkered history in recent years: alternatively being acclaimed as a panacea and banned as a health hazard. Internally it was once widely used by herbalists for coughs, stomach ulceration, and digestive upsets, while externally it is excellent for treating bruises, sprains, and even fractures. It encourages cell growth, so it can speed up the repair of wounds and traumatic injuries. CAUTIONS Use is restricted in many countries as comfrey contains known carcinogens, although it is debatable how much of these are present in extracts; do not use on dirty wounds, or it may lead to abscesses.

OTHER HERBS THAT MAY BE HELPFUL
snakeroot (p.178) ● burdock (p.67) ● turmeric (p.130) ● Du Huo (p.153)
● Gui Zhi (p.129) ● tabasco pepper (p.128) ● ginger (p.185)
● sweet flag (p.51) ● dandelion (p.87) ● bedstraw (p.57) ● asafetida (p.95)

Arthritis

CELERY SEEDS

Arthritis simply means "joint inflammation"—but there are various types of arthritis and exact diagnosis is important in each case.

Osteoarthritis is the sort of "wear-and-tear" variety that afflicts as many as 52 percent of older people. Causes include sports injury or obesity, putting excess strain on a joint. Typically in osteoarthritis the protective cartilage between the bones of a joint becomes damaged and wears away, causing the bones to rub together and become deformed. Joints often creak and become stiff and painful. Movement of the joint is frequently limited. Orthodox treatment usually involves anti-inflammatory drugs or eventual joint-replacement surgery.

Rheumatoid arthritis is a more serious and potentially crippling disease, which may be related to hereditary health problems or autoimmune disease, or—most frequently—be of unknown cause. Here the membranous capsule covering the joint (the synovium) becomes thickened and inflamed, leading eventually to painful destruction of cartilage and bone. The end result can be severe bone deformity.

Western herbalists tend to see arthritis as a toxic problem—most obviously in gout, where the problem relates to excess

ARTHRITIS DIET

Western herbalists usually recommend arthritics to avoid foods that leave acidic residues, such as red meat, refined (white) sugars, and dairy products, as well as acidic fruits and vegetables, such as tomatoes, oranges, strawberries, spinach, rhubarb, and sorrel.

uric acid collecting in joints; waste products linger in the body and eventually oxidize and damage delicate membranes. Treatment usually focuses on blood-cleansing herbs, diuretics, and digestive stimulants, with anti-inflammatory herbs being employed in order to provide symptomatic relief.

In Chinese theory arthritis is seen initially as attack by a combination of "external evils": osteoarthritis, for example, is usually a cold-damp-wind problem with a shifting pattern of aches and twinges; symptoms are usually worse when the weather is cold and wet. Rheumatoid arthritis can be an excess heat problem. Both types are described as "Bi syndrome" (with Bi meaning pain).

ALOE VERA

In ayurvedic theory arthritis is associated with toxic vata (amavata), since the bones (asthi) are most closely associated with this humor. As in the Western herbal approach, it can be linked to sluggish digestion leading to a build-up of waste products. Treatment of osteoarthritis often involves a pitta-promoting diet with hot spices to encourage agni (digestive fire) and burn off the toxic ama. "Hot" gemstones, such as rubies or garnets set in gold, are also worn.

Ayurveda subdivides arthritis into pitta, vata, and kapha types, with rheumatoid arthritis being most similar to the pitta type. This is treated with cooling, bitter herbs—such as aloe vera—rather than the pitta-promoting remedies that are recommended for osteoarthritis (vata- or kapha-types); sandalwood or gotu kola is used in medicated oils for external massage.

APIUM GRAVEOLENS Celery

PARTS USED *seeds, essential oil* TASTE *bitter, sweet*
CHARACTER *cool* MERIDIANS *kidney, liver, urinary bladder*
ACTIONS *antirheumatic, sedative, urinary antiseptic,
antispasmodic, diuretic, carminative, hypotensive, some
antifungal activity*

USES Celery is diuretic and is often used for fluid-
retention problems. It is also a specific for encouraging
the excretion of uric acid, so it is helpful in arthritic
conditions, especially gout, where urate crystals in the
joints contribute to inflammation. The root was once
used for urinary stones, although now we tend to use
mainly the seeds, while a juice made from the stalks
has some tonic action for debilitated conditions.
CAUTIONS Celery seed contains bergapten, which can
increase the photosensitivity of the skin; avoid the oil
and large doses of seed in pregnancy.

FUCUS VESICULOSIS/ Bladderwrack/*Kun Bu*
LAMINARIA SPP.

PARTS USED *whole plant* TASTE *salty* CHARACTER *cold*
MERIDIANS *spleen, stomach, kidney* ACTIONS *nutritive, thyroid
tonic, antirheumatic, anti-inflammatory*

USES Various seaweeds are used medicinally, including
bladderwrack *(F. vesiculosis)* and kelp or *Kun Bu*
(Laminaria spp.*)*. All are salty, tonic herbs, rich in iodine
and trace metals and a good source of essential
nutrients. The iodine content stimulates the thyroid and
speeds up body metabolism—hence their reputation as
slimming aids. The Chinese use *Kun Bu* to reduce
nodules and swellings and regard it as a kidney tonic
to encourage urination and clear excess phlegm and
dampness. Externally, infused oils can be used for
rheumatic and arthritic problems.
CAUTIONS Bladderwrack concentrates toxic waste metals
and should not be collected in contaminated areas.

HARPAGOPHYTUM PROCUMBENS Devil's claw

PARTS USED *tuber* TASTE *bitter* CHARACTER *warm* MERIDIANS *liver, spleen* ACTIONS *anti-inflammatory, antirheumatic, analgesic, sedative, diuretic, digestive stimulant*

USES Devil's claw is a native of the Kalahari desert and reputedly came to the attention of Westerners when a Boer farmer noticed the native Bushmen gathering the roots to treat digestive upsets and rheumatism. The plant was sent to Germany for investigation and by the late 1950s its anti-inflammatory and antirheumatic properties were well established. Studies suggest that taking the herb for at least six weeks can significantly improve the movement of arthritic joints and reduce swelling. Devil's claw can also be used as a bitter digestive stimulant for liver and gall-bladder disorders.

CAUTIONS Avoid in pregnancy as it is believed to stimulate uterine contractions; avoid in cases of gastric or duodenal ulcer.

RUMEX CRISPUS Curly dock

PARTS USED *root* TASTE *bitter, astringent* CHARACTER *cold, dry* MERIDIANS *kidney, large intestine* ACTIONS *laxative, bile stimulant, cleansing*

USES Curly dock is a cleansing herb suitable for chronic skin problems and arthritic complaints. It helps to clear toxins and acts as a gentle stimulant for the liver and kidneys. It is also laxative and stimulates bile flow, but is rather gentler than strong purgatives such as rhubarb, so it is one of the more suitable remedies for use in pregnancy. Curly dock can also be used as a blood tonic in anemia and is a lymphatic cleanser, useful for swollen glands. It is an astringent remedy and may be used for wounds.

CAUTIONS Avoid regular or prolonged use in pregnancy and when breastfeeding.

OTHER HERBS THAT MAY BE HELPFUL
eucalyptus (p.197) ● *rosemary (p.71)* ● *curly dock (p.151)*
● *meadowsweet (p.184)* ● *snakeroot (p.178)* ● *bladderwrack (p.150)*
● *tabasco pepper (p.128)* ● *St.-John's-wort (p.111)*

EUCALYPTUS

Rheumatic or muscular aches and pains

Rheumatism is a very imprecise term used to describe the aches and pains suffered in muscles. The label can encompass fibrositis (inflammation of the muscle sheath) and lumbago (low back pain) and is used interchangeably with "myalgia," meaning pain in the muscles.

Orthodox medicine will generally prescribe painkillers, while the herbal approach usually involves the use of cleansing herbs to remove any chemical toxins lingering in the tissues. Diuretics, digestive stimulants, circulatory stimulants, and laxatives are all likely to be found in Western herbal remedies for rheumatism. Herbal anti-inflammatories and painkillers may also be included. External warming remedies to stimulate the circulation by encouraging blood flow to a particular area are widely used. In China, plasters soaked in stimulating oils such as eucalyptus or camphor are popular.

In Chinese theory the muscles are linked to the spleen, so persistent rheumatism is likely to be associated with a deficiency in spleen energy and with problems in separating the Jin (clear) and Ye (turbid) products of digestion, leading to a build-up of toxins in the tissues.

In ayurveda muscles (mamsa) are associated with kapha (water), so muscle problems may be associated with kapha imbalance and are more likely to occur in damp climates. They are treated with warm, drying herbs as well as low-kapha diets (avoiding excess sweet foods, refined carbohydrates, and so on).

ANGELICA PUBESCENS Pubescent angelica/*Du Huo*

PARTS USED *root* TASTE *pungent, bitter* CHARACTER *slightly warm* MERIDIANS *kidney, urinary bladder* ACTIONS *antirheumatic, analgesic, anti-inflammatory, sedative, hypotensive, nervous stimulant*

USES *Du Huo* is primarily used to combat attack by the external pathogens wind and damp, so it is helpful for superficial syndromes, including colds, rheumatism, and *Bi* syndrome (arthritis). It is used especially for "wind-damp" problems affecting the the lower back and legs, which may manifest as cramping pains, dull aches, or stiffness.It is also used for headaches and toothache associated with "wind-damp." It is frequently combined with *Ma Huang* for "wind-cold" where there are generalized aches and pains but no obvious fever.
CAUTIONS Avoid in "deficient *Yin*" and excess fire syndromes.

SALIX ALBA White willow

PARTS USED *bark* TASTE *astringent, bitter* CHARACTER *cool, dry* MERIDIANS *urinary bladder, kidney, heart* ACTIONS *antirheumatic, anti-inflammatory, antipyretic, antihidrotic, analgesic, antiseptic, astringent, bitter digestive tonic*

USES In European tradition the silver-leaved willow was associated with the moon and regarded as cooling for inflammatory disorders. It is effective for clearing heat, especially from the joints, throat, eyes, and urinary tract, and is good as a general treatment for headaches. The *Salix* genus gives its name to salicylates—the group of anti-inflammatory compounds that are familiar in aspirin and present in significant amounts in the bark and leaves of white willow. The plant is used for relieving pain and reducing fever and is helpful for rheumatism, gout, arthritis, feverish chills, and headaches.
CAUTIONS Avoid in cases of salicylate allergy.

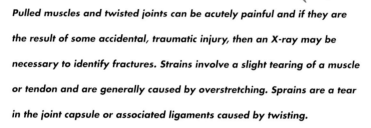

OTHER HERBS THAT MAY BE HELPFUL
arnica (p.146) ● comfrey (p.147) ● devil's claw (p.151)
● St.John's-wort (p.111) ● camphor (p.157) ● rosemary (p.71)

ROSEMARY

Strains, sprains, and tendon problems

Pulled muscles and twisted joints can be acutely painful and if they are the result of some accidental, traumatic injury, then an X-ray may be necessary to identify fractures. Strains involve a slight tearing of a muscle or tendon and are generally caused by overstretching. Sprains are a tear in the joint capsule or associated ligaments caused by twisting.

Treatment for traumatic injuries like these generally involves analgesic and anti-inflammatory herbs applied in ointments or poultices. Alternating heat and cold can help to bring out bruises and encourage healing: the injured joint needs to be soaked for three or four minutes in hot water containing heating herbs such as pepper, rosemary, or camphor, followed by immersion in iced water, repeated for as long as is bearable.

In Chinese theory tendons are associated with the liver, so persistent problems may require liver tonics as well as topical applications—this is especially true of knee disorders. Tennis elbow involves inflammation of the tendons and usually follows excessive use of the forearm muscles— but liver herbs are also worth adding to the remedy. Frozen shoulder is a chronic stiffness of the shoulder joint, usually with no obvious cause; it is generally treated as arthritis. It may also be related to stress and tension and with a suppressed desire to "hit out" at whatever is causing the problem.

HERBAL INFUSION

HAMAMELIS VIRGINIANUM   Witch-hazel

PARTS USED *leaves, branches, bark* TASTE *bitter, pungent, astringent* CHARACTER *cool, dry* MERIDIANS *liver* ACTIONS *astringent, stops internal and external bleeding, anti-inflammatory*

USES Virginian witch-hazel was widely used by the Native North Americans: the Menomees rubbed the decoction into their legs to keep them supple during sports, while the Potawatomis put twigs into sweat-baths to relieve sore muscles. Today witch-hazel is a familiar first-aid remedy for bruises, sprains, cuts, and grazes. It is still commonly used to ease varicose veins and piles, is applied to spots and blemishes, and is valuable for many minor injuries. It is also used internally for diarrhea, colitis, excessive menstruation, and hemorrhage.

CAUTIONS None noted.

SIDA CORDIFOLIA   *bala*

PARTS USED *root* TASTE *sweet* CHARACTER *cooling* MERIDIANS *kidney, heart* ACTIONS *tonic, rejuvenative, aphrodisiac, demulcent, diuretic, stimulant, nervine, analgesic, wound healer*

USES Various members of the mallow family are used in ayurveda in a variety of ways; among which *bala* is one of the most versatile. It is a heart and nerve tonic and is helpful for all sorts of *vata* disorders, for mental problems and paralysis. It is very soothing for arthritic and muscular pains and is used externally in medicated oils for both muscle cramps and neuralgia. Taken in a milk decoction, it is helpful in debility and weakness and promotes tissue healing in infectious diseases. It is combined with black pepper or ginger for chronic fevers.

CAUTIONS Avoid in excess *kapha* syndromes and high *ama* conditions.

155

OTHER HERBS THAT MAY BE HELPFUL
He Shou Wu (p.179) ● *walnut (p.165)* ● *Du Zhong (p.164)* ●
cinnamon (p.129) ● *white willow (p.153)* ● *devil's claw (p.151)*
● *comfrey (p.147)* ● *arnica (p.146)* ● *Du Huo (p.153)*

CINNAMON

Backache

Backache can cover a multitude of ills—from muscular

aches and pains (lumbago and fibrositis) and problems

with the sciatic nerve to pains associated with kidney

disorders or a displaced uterus. Identifying the cause of persistent

backache is important, as different types require different treatment.

Holistic therapies place great emphasis on accompanying symptoms and

history—tinnitus or ear problems suggest kidney weakness; pain

radiating to the foot, sciatica; recent overexertion, pulled muscles. Muscle

problems are generally treated as for rheumatism (p.152).

SYZYGIUM AROMATICUM   Cloves/*Ding Xiang*/*lavanga*

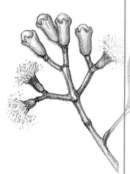

PARTS USED *flower buds, essential oil* TASTE *pungent*
CHARACTER *warm* MERIDIANS *spleen, stomach, kidney*
ACTIONS *antiseptic, carminative, mild local anesthetic,
warming stimulant, analgesic, anti-emetic, antiparasitic*

USES Cloves are a useful remedy for nausea and
digestive upsets, and are warming for colds. The oil
makes a good emergency first-aid remedy for
toothache and can relieve insect bites. The Chinese
regard cloves as a good tonic for kidney *Yang*, helpful
for the reproductive organs and for deficient kidney
syndromes, which are often characterized by low back
pain. The herb is also used for hiccups, nausea, and
vomiting associated with cold in the stomach or
ascending spleen or stomach *Qi*. In ayurveda cloves
are regarded as *tajasic*, but are also a lung remedy.
CAUTIONS Avoid in "deficient *Yin*" with heat symptoms.

CINNAMOMUM CAMPHORA Camphor/*Zhang Nao*/*karpura*

PARTS USED *crystallized distilled oil* TASTE *pungent, bitter* CHARACTER *hot* MERIDIANS *heart* ACTIONS *expectorant, nasal decongestant, stimulant, antispasmodic, nervine, analgesic, antiseptic*

USES Camphor is used in ayurvedic medicine to open the senses and clear the mind. It is often combined with sesame oil as a massage to help meditation and is burned in incense to purify the atmosphere and encourage devotion and worship. In India a pinch of powdered camphor is taken like snuff as a nasal decongestant and for headaches; the infusion is also taken internally for a range of respiratory problems and emotional upsets. It is never used internally in the West —especially since it is known to contain safrole, which is carcinogenic. Instead it is traditionally used in medicated chest rubs for coughs, influenza, bronchitis, and breathing difficulties and for muscular aches and pains. In aromatherapy it is used to stimulate heart and respiration and to raise low blood pressure. A compress soaked in a weak camphor infusion can relieve backache, and the herb is used in lotions for cold sores and chilblains. In China camphor is primarily used like smelling salts to combat fainting and coma and is also a popular ingredient in external plasters and rubs for traumatic injuries, sprains, and strains. Camphorated oil can be made by dissolving 1oz/25g of camphor crystals in 1pt/500ml of sesame oil.

CAUTIONS Do not take internally and use only pure raw camphor, not synthetic substitutes; avoid in "deficient *Qi*," insomnia, and pregnancy; overdosage can lead to a sore throat and loss of appetite.

Holistic health tips

• Passive exercise can be helpful for arthritic joints. With the help of a partner if need be, flex the affected joint manually so that no effort is actually made by the joint itself. Repeat up to 20 times each session and repeat daily.

• Hot and cold treatments can help with traumatic injuries such as sprains and bruising. Fill one large basin with very hot water and plenty of fresh rosemary sprigs or 50 drops of rosemary oil. Fill another basin with cold water, plenty of ice, and several handfuls of lavender flowers or 50 drops of lavender oil. Then soak the affected joint/limb alternately in the two basins for as long as you can bear. Keep this up for an hour or more if possible to encourage healing and ease pains.

• Diet plays an important part in treating chronic aches and pains such as arthritis, gout, and lumbago. Foods that leave an acid residue can encourage the build-up of toxins in the joints. These include foods that are high in organic acid (such as citrus fruit, tomatoes, spinach, and strawberries) as well as red meat. Avoid all these as much as possible.

• Food intolerance can also lead to arthritic conditions: try an exclusion diet avoiding each likely allergen in turn for two weeks. Top of the suspect list are usually cow's milk, wheat, members of the Solanaceae family (bell peppers, aubergines, potatoes, tomatoes, etc.), and beef.

GENITOURINARY SYSTEM
Western Approach

The orthodox Western melding of reproductive and urinary problems into a single "genitourinary" category rather typifies the mechanistic approach that conventional medicine takes. The organs (especially in men) happen to be anatomically close together, so they tend to be treated together —although in most cases the reproductive and sexual problems have little to do with excretion and water metabolism.

Male reproductive problems are often sidelined into urinary-tract issues, with little emphasis on the emotional or energy issues involved; prostate problems, for example, are usually seen as a natural and inevitable consequence of aging, to be treated with surgery, which often has to be repeated. A more holistic approach, however, regards prostate problems as associated with energy stagnation and lethargy. Physical inactivity seems to trigger the condition, especially in the newly retired: as a result, creative energies and vigor seem to stagnate and decline.

Similarly menstrual problems (especially fibroids and endometriosis, which can involve heavy/irregular bleeding) are usually treated by hysterectomy. This simply removes the symptoms, but often leaves behind energy imbalances and stagnation, which cause further emotional and physical problems. Herbalists use a variety of remedies—many now known to have a hormonal action—to normalize function.

Above *Keeping active is important to maintain energy and vigor, and may help to hold prostate problems at bay.*

Below *Chaste-tree is a valuable herb for gynecological problems.*

159

Above Dang Gui *(Chinese angelica root) is a good gynecological tonic and is much used in the West.*

Below *Lustrous hair is a sign of healthy* Jing*. This is stored in the kidney, where part is transformed into* Qi*.*

In Chinese theory the two most important organs associated with reproductive and gynecological problems are the kidney and liver; energy weakness or imbalance here is blamed for many problems that Westerners label "genitourinary."

The liver is where blood is "stored," so it tends to be closely associated with menstruation. Liver tonics, such as *Dang Gui*, are important gynecological herbs used for a range of problems.

The kidney stores vital essence or *Jing*. Part of this *Jing* can be transformed into kidney *Qi*, which also affects our energy and aging processes. Traditional theory maintains that the *Jing* stored in the kidney is transformed into bone marrow, which spreads along the spinal cord to the brain—itself originally believed to be made of bone marrow. Through this connection with the bones and brain the kidney is also associated with head hair—an abundance of lustrous hair is believed to indicate healthy kidney *Qi* and thus strong essence and creativity. The kidney is also associated with the ears, so deafness and tinnitus—like graying hair and hair loss—are outward signs of the kidney's energy and *Jing* store: all are common occurrences as we age and as kidney *Jing* weakens, so kidney tonics are especially important, both at the menopause and for older patients.

Urinary function or "water metabolism" is associated in Chinese theory with the spleen, so problems here are likely to be treated with digestive remedies rather than relying solely on the urinary antiseptics and the diuretics of orthodox medicine.

GENITOURINARY SYSTEM
Ayurvedic Approach

Ayurvedic medicine similarly makes a distinction between reproductive disorders and urinary problems: the latter are clearly related to water metabolism and humoral imbalance, while reproductive problems are associated with sexual energies and vigor.

The *chakras* (energy centers) play an important role in maintaining vitality and, where reproductive problems are concerned, the first or root *chakra* is especially relevant. This is located at the base of the spine but is also associated with the womb. It also helps our sense of "rootedness"—a feeling of belonging or earthing. In women who have had a hysterectomy, this *chakra* can be damaged and there is a risk that they may lose this sense of "earthing" and have problems concentrating or maintaining sustained interest in anything; emotional behavior might become erratic and unsettled as well.

Above *The ayurvedic view is that in both sexes the suppression of sexual energy can weaken vitality.*

Below *Yoga offers a way of maintaining balance and energy levels.*

Ayurvedic philosophy is influenced by Indian tantric beliefs in the power of sexual energy and its role in meditation and mental vigor: instead of the guilt associated with sexual performance in traditional Western societies (and reinforced in the past by many religious practices), sexual activity is seen as simply another dimension of normal vitality. Abstinence is sometimes seen as a cause of disease, just as too much can lead to debility and exhaustion. Repressing sexual energy is regarded as likely to cause stagnation and weaken vitality—additional meditation and yoga practice are seen as essential to replace the vitality created by sexual activity in those who choose celibacy.

OTHER HERBS THAT MAY BE HELPFUL
cinnamon (p.129) ● Nu Zhen Zi (p.121) ● He Shou Wu (p.179)
● horse-tail (p.184) ● agrimony (p.192) ● celery (p.150)

Kidney problems

*In Western medicine the kidney is regarded
as little more than a filter, extracting useful
chemicals from the urine before sending it on its way. Kidney disorders
largely involve infection, inflammation, and tissue damage, which
interfere with this important function.*

*Urinary gravel, for example, is formed from deposits of either uric acid
or calcium salts, which crystallize from solution when the urine is highly
concentrated. They then collect in the kidney and urinary tract, blocking
the tiny tubes and causing extreme pain—renal calculi (stones) may cause
sufferers to double up in agony. Orthodox treatment may involve surgery,
but the stones can often be dispersed by means of professional herbal
treatment—using herbs such as marshmallow or cornsilk with
horse-tail to help repair the damage that has been
caused. Kidney infections will often respond to
echinacea, while many herbs are classified as
"urinary antiseptics" to help cleanse the kidney
and urinary tract of infections and toxins.
Chinese medicine also regards the kidney as
having prime responsibility for regulating water
metabolism, although it has a number of equally vital
other functions. In Chinese theory "body fluids" are divided into
"clear fluid," which circulates through the organs and tissues, and "turbid
fluid," which is transformed into sweat and urine and is then excreted*

CORNSILK

ECHINACEA FLOWER

THE KIDNEYS

The body's two kidneys are located in the lower back, on either side of the spine just below the diaphragm. Each contains thousands of nephrons that filter waste products (such as urea) from the blood, excreting them from the body as urine. It is possible to live a normal life with only one healthy kidney.

from the body. The kidney helps separate the two and sends the clear fluid upward and the turbid fluid downward for disposal. It also helps to direct the Qi flow downward, thus aiding the work of the lung during inhalation and generally coordinating respiration.

If kidney Qi is weak, it can lead to breathing problems and to certain types of asthma; this explains why respiratory disorders are sometimes treated in Chinese medicine with kidney-strengthening herbs. Many different herbs are available to strengthen kidney Qi, Yin, Yang, and Jing.

In ayurvedic theory the kidneys are believed to be mainly involved in water metabolism, with toxins (ama) lodging in the tract and leading to infection (a pitta condition) and stones. Water is believed to bring rather more than just fluid into the body: it also brings prana—the life force—so drinking aerated or spring water (rather than distilled or heavily chlorinated water) is vital. Too much water, however, is believed to weaken the body, as it drains essential substances from the tissues to be excreted. Cold water is believed to be especially damaging for the kidneys, as it increases kapha levels within the body. Excessive use of diuretics can also be damaging, as these are thought to aggravate vata (air) and overstimulate kidney action.

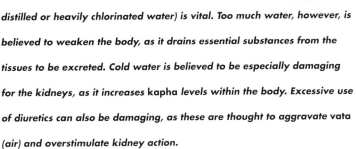

WATER

CORNUS OFFICINALIS Dogwood/*Shan Zhu Yu*

PARTS USED *fruit* **TASTE** *sour* **CHARACTER** *warm*
MERIDIANS *liver, kidney* **ACTIONS** *antibacterial, antifungal, diuretic, hypotensive*

USES *Shan Zhu Yu* has been used since about AD 200 to replenish liver and kidney *Jing*; it was included in the *Shen Nong Ben Cao Jing*, the herbal credited to the mythological Shen Nong. It is also regarded as an astringent herb to stop bleeding and excessive sweating. It is employed for urinary dysfunction associated with kidney weakness, although as a *Jing* tonic it is also included in remedies for scanty menstruation and for menopausal problems.

CAUTIONS Avoid if there is painful or difficult urination and use cautiously in "deficient kidney *Yang*" syndromes; *Shan Zhu Yu* should not be combined with *Jie Geng.*

EUCOMMIA ULMOIDES *Du Zhong*

PARTS USED *bark* **TASTE** *sweet* **CHARACTER** *warm*
MERIDIANS *liver, kidney* **ACTIONS** *diuretic, hypotensive, reduces cholesterol levels, sedative, uterine relaxant*

USES *Du Zhong* is the only surviving member of its genus and was first collected in the 1880s. Extracts have been used in recent years to treat high blood pressure, although in TCM it is regarded more as a tonic for liver and kidney *Qi*; it also smooths the flow of *Qi* and blood to strengthen bones and muscles. It is used for kidney weakness characterized by low back pain, frequent urination, impotence, and weakness in the lower part of the body and is often combined with *Bu Gu Zhi* for "deficient kidney *Yang*" or with *Gui Zhi* and *Du Huo* for problems associated with "cold-damp."

CAUTIONS Avoid in "deficient *Yin*" and if there are active fire symptoms.

JUGLANS REGIA Walnut/*Hu Tao Ren*

PARTS USED *seeds (nut kernel)* TASTE *sweet* CHARACTER *warm* MERIDIANS *lung, kidney, large intestine* ACTIONS *astringent, laxative, anti-inflammatory, mild hypoglycemic, nutrient, dissolves urinary stones*

USES In the West walnuts are valued as a gentle nutrient and digestive remedy, while the nut oil is a good source of essential fatty acids. In China the nuts are regarded more as a *Yang* tonic, helpful for the kidneys and to warm and strengthen lung *Qi*. The nuts are often used for symptoms of kidney deficiency—typically low back pain and urinary dysfunction. Walnut is valuable for constipation in the elderly (often with *Huo Ma Ren* and other herbs) and is combined with *Ren Shen* for lung deficiency problems.

CAUTIONS Avoid in heat, phlegm or fire syndromes and "deficient *Yin*."

PSORALEA CORYLIFOLIA *Bu Gu Zi*

PARTS USED *fruit, seed* TASTE *pungent, bitter* CHARACTER *warm* MERIDIANS *kidney, spleen* ACTIONS *antibacterial, vasodilator, anti-tumour, uterine stimulant, haemostatic*

USES *Bu Gu Zi* is mainly used in China as a *Yang* tonic for the kidneys and as an astringent to stop bleeding. The herb is often used for problems associated with kidney weakness, such as impotence, low back pain, and urinary dysfunction. The Chinese associate "cock-crow diarrhea"—the urgent need to pass stools at dawn—with spleen and kidney weakness, and *Bu Gu Zhi* is the standard remedy, used with herbs like nutmeg (p.91), *Wu Wei Zi* (p.181), and ginger (p.185). It is also included in the delightfully named *Qing E Wan*—the "blue fairy lady pills for lumbago"—which also contain garlic, walnut, and *Du Zhong* in equal amounts.

CAUTIONS May increase the photosensitivity of the skin.

OTHER HERBS THAT MAY BE HELPFUL
celery (p.150) ● *white deadnettle (p.170)* ● *horse-tail (p.184)*
● *agrimony (p.192)* ● *yarrow (p.133)* ● *dandelion (p.87)*
● *lady's-mantle (p.173)*

CELERY

Urinary disorders

*Common urinary problems are generally associated
with inflammation, which is usually caused by infection.
Cystitis simply means inflammation of the bladder,
while urethritis is inflammation of the urethra (the tube
connecting the bladder with the outside world). The first is more
common in women, since their urethras are much shorter than
men's: around 1½in/3.5cm compared with about 8in/20cm in men.*

Cystitis affects around half of all women at some point during their
lives, with typical symptoms including increased frequency of urination,
pain, or a burning sensation when passing urine and a dull ache in the
lower abdomen. Men may have difficulty in urinating in urethritis. Like all
opportunist infections, the bacteria causing the problem are more likely to
attack when sufferers are tired, overworked, or under stress. Making the
urine more alkaline can help: so limit meat intake, avoid acidic foods, such
as rhubarb, oranges, and pickles, and opt for more vegetarian dishes.

In ayurveda acute urinary-tract infections are due to high pitta and are
treated with anti-pitta herbs and diets (avoiding alcohol and spices), with
a reduction in sexual activity also recommended. Difficulties with urination
may be associated with poor kidney function as well as an imbalance in
the humors: vata problems generally involve colicky pains and backache;
in pitta conditions the urine is dark—possibly tinged with blood—and
there is a fever; while in kapha conditions urine is pale or milky with
mucus and dull abdominal pains.

ALISMA PLANTAGO-AQUATICA Water-plantain/*Ze Xie*

PARTS USED *tuber* TASTE *sweet* CHARACTER *cold*
MERIDIANS *kidney, urinary bladder* ACTIONS *antibacterial,
diuretic, hypotensive, hypoglycemic, reduces cholesterol levels*

USES *Ze Xie* is used in Chinese medicine in order to
regulate water metabolism, resolve dampness, and
eliminate "heat and dampness in the lower *Jiao*." It was
listed in the *Shen Nong Ban Cao Jing* and is used
mainly for edema and urinary dysfunction that is
associated with poor water metabolism and damp. It is
also used to prevent the production of "kidney fire,"
which may result from "deficient kidney *Yin* with heat
syndrome," where symptoms generally include tinnitus
and vertigo as well as urinary dysfunction and
back pain.

CAUTIONS Avoid in "deficient kidney *Yang*."

COIX LACHRYMA-JOBI Job's tears/*Yi Yi Ren*

PARTS USED *seeds* TASTE *sweet, bland* CHARACTER *slightly
cold* MERIDIANS *spleen, stomach, lung, large intestine, kidney*
ACTIONS *analgesic, febrifugal, sedative, hypoglycemic,
antitumor*

USES *Yi Yi Ren* is another herb dating back to the days
of Shen Nong; in China it is often used rather like pearl
barley and made into *congees* (porridge) as a
household remedy for diarrhea and digestive upsets,
and for excessive or difficult urination. The herb is
traditionally taken to regulate water metabolism, so it
helps to tonify spleen and combat diarrhea. It is also
used for spasmodic pains and arthritis, and for clearing
pus in abscesses. It is combined with *Fu Ling* (p.169)
and *Bai Zhu* (p.78) for diarrhea that is associated with
spleen deficiency.

CAUTIONS Use with care in pregnancy.

PETROSELINUM CRISPUM Parsley

PARTS USED *leaves, roots, seeds* TASTE *bitter, pungent*
CHARACTER *neutral, dry* MERIDIANS *urinary bladder, kidney,
liver* ACTIONS *antispasmodic, antirheumatic, diuretic,
carminative, expectorant, tonic, antimicrobial, nutrient*

USES Like other plants with a tendency to "rob the soil,"
parsley is a good source of vitamins (especially A, C,
and E) and minerals, so it makes a useful addition to
the diet in iron-deficient anemia. It is a diuretic, often
used for cystitis, as well as fluid retention associated
with PMS; it will also stimulate menstrual flow and can
help relieve menopausal symptoms. Crushed leaves
were once used as a breast poultice to help reduce
milk flow in nursing mothers. Parsley seed is a useful
cleansing remedy in rheumatism, gout, and arthritis.
CAUTIONS Avoid therapeutic doses in pregnancy and
kidney inflammations; excessive doses of the seed are
toxic: do not exceed 10ml of 1:5 tincture per dose.

TRIBULIS TERRESTRIS *Ci Ji Li/gokshura*

PARTS USED *fruit* TASTE *pungent, bitter* CHARACTER *neutral*
MERIDIANS *liver* ACTIONS *rejuvenative and aphrodisiac tonic,
diuretic, analgesic, clears urinary stones*

USES *Gokshura* is an important remedy for urinary-tract
problems, including stones, cystitis, and infections. It
also strengthens kidney function, so is a good tonic for
the reproductive system. In ayurveda it is classified as
sattvic, so it has a calming effect on the nervous system
and is often used with *ashwaganda* as a rejuvenating
mixture, or with dry ginger as an analgesic for nerve
pains. In Chinese medicine it is used for restoring liver
Yang (linked to high blood pressure and headaches).
CAUTIONS Avoid in dehydration, pregnancy, and in *Qi*
and blood-deficiency syndromes.

VACCINIUM OXYCOCCOS Small cranberry

PARTS USED *berries, juice* TASTE *astringent, sour*
CHARACTER *cold, dry* MERIDIANS *urinary bladder, spleen,
stomach* ACTIONS *antiscorbutic, urinary antiseptic, diuretic*

USES Until comparatively recently cranberries were
regarded medicinally as, at best, little more than a
useful source of vitamin C. However, research in the
early 1990s in the USA indicated that unsweetened
cranberry juice has a significant effect on urinary
bacteria. As a result, the juice started to be used
for urinary infections and cystitis. Quite high doses
of unsweetened cranberry juice are needed (e.g.
8fl oz/225ml, taken every hour for up to ten hours).
Cranberries also show some hypoglycemic activity, so
they have been promoted as a remedy for late-onset
diabetes; they remain an excellent source of vitamin C.
CAUTIONS None indicated.

WOLFIPORIA COCOS *Fu Ling*

PARTS USED *sclerotium of the fungus (usually found on
pine-tree roots)* TASTE *sweet, neutral* CHARACTER *neutral*
MERIDIANS *lung, spleen, heart, urinary bladder*
ACTIONS *diuretic, sedative, hypoglycemic*

USES *Fu Ling*, one of the many fungi used in Chinese
medicine, is an effective diuretic—traditionally said to
"clear dampness and regulate water metabolism," and
used for problems such as scanty urination, edema,
and painful urinary dysfunction. It also strengthens the
spleen, stomach, and middle *Jiao*; transforms phlegm;
has a calming effect on the heart and *Shen* (spirit); and
is useful for palpitations and insomnia. It is used with
Chen Pi where phlegm and fluid problems lead to
abdominal bloating, vomiting, or diarrhea.
CAUTIONS Avoid in excessive urination or prolapse of
the urogenital organs.

169

OTHER HERBS THAT MAY BE HELPFUL
cornsilk (p.199) ● *echinacea (p.45)* ● *Siberian ginseng (p.109)*
● *walnut (p.165)* ● *Nu Zhen Zi (p.121)* ● *gokshura (p.168)*
● *bala (p.155)* ● *marshmallow (p.78)* ● *agrimony (p.192)*

WALNUT

Prostate problems

Men are often reluctant to seek help for health

problems, especially for disorders of the reproductive system. The prostate

gland is one of the male sex organs and produces an alkaline fluid that is

contained in semen. With age the gland often becomes enlarged, causing

problems in passing water: the flow is reduced and residual urine remains

in the bladder, leading to infection. Urine can also travel back from the

bladder to the kidneys and cause damage and reduced kidney function.

Orthodox treatment involves removing part of the prostate gland, while

herbal remedies concentrate on restoring the body's chemical balance by

reducing production of dihydrotestosterone (DHT) and combating resulting

infections. Energizing tonics for kidney Qi may also help.

LAMIUM ALBUM   White deadnettle

PARTS USED *aerial parts collected while flowering*
TASTE *astringent, bitter* CHARACTER *hot* MERIDIANS *liver,
kidney* ACTIONS *anti-inflammatory, antispasmodic, astringent,
diuretic, expectorant, menstrual regulator, styptic, wound healer*

USES White deadnettle is used mainly for menstrual and
urinary disorders: deadnettle tea can be helpful for
cystitis and prostatitis (inflammation of the prostate) and
to speed up recovery after surgery for an enlarged
prostate. It may also be taken for heavy periods and
used as a douche for vaginal discharges, as well as
other high-mucus conditions, such as mucous colitis or
nasal catarrh. Externally white deadnettle creams and
ointments can be used on cuts, grazes, and minor burns.
CAUTIONS None noted.

SERENOA REPENS Saw palmetto

PARTS USED *fruits* TASTE *sweet, pungent, astringent*
CHARACTER *warm, dry* MERIDIANS *kidney, spleen*
ACTIONS *tonic, diuretic, sedative, urinary antiseptic, endocrine stimulant, hormonal action*

USES Saw palmetto berries were valued by the Native North Americans for their tonic effect and taken as a strengthening remedy in debility. The herb was traditionally used for cystitis and prostate problems, and in recent years has been shown to prevent the conversion of the male hormone testosterone into DHT (believed to be responsible for benign prostate enlargement). Saw palmetto also encourages the breakdown of any DHT that may have formed, thus helping both to prevent and cure the problem. It is often included in products aimed at improving male libido, as well as in general tonics, usually targeted at older men. It can help to increase weight and strength, and may encourage breast development in women.
CAUTIONS None noted.

TURNERA DIFFUSA VAR. APHRODISIACA Damiana

PARTS USED *leaves* TASTE *pungent, bitter* CHARACTER *heating*
MERIDIANS *kidney* ACTIONS *stimulant, tonic, antidepressant, laxative, diuretic, aphrodisiac, testosterogenic, urinary antiseptic*

USES Damiana acts as a tonic for the nervous system and as an antidepressant, but is also stimulating for the digestion and urinary system, useful in convalescence. It can be helpful in prostatitis and urinary-tract infections. Although largely regarded as a potent male aphrodisiac and used for treating impotence and infertility, it can be helpful for various menstrual disorders as well. Damiana is used with vervain and oats for depression and anxiety states, or with betony and oats for confusion and debility in the elderly.
CAUTIONS None noted.

OTHER HERBS THAT MAY BE HELPFUL
marigold (p.63) ● Atlantic yam (p.79) ● St.John's-wort (p.111)
● raspberry (p.185) ● mugwort (p.112) ● Bai Shao Yao (p.86)
● Shu Di Huang (p.53)

ST. JOHN'S-WORT

Menstrual problems

Herbs have for centuries been a vital standby for a vast array of female health problems, as names such as motherwort and lady's-mantle imply. In modern Western medicine many gynecological problems are blamed on hormonal imbalance, with the result that potent remedies, such as the contraceptive pill, are prescribed to young teenagers to help regulate their periods. Many traditional women's herbs have been shown to have a hormonal action, acting on the ovaries or the pituitary gland; other herbs are uterine stimulants and tonics, used to strengthen the womb and combat both the discomfort of period pain and the exertions of labor.

In Chinese theory the liver is closely linked with the menstrual cycle, as it is believed to store blood and to regulate its release into the body as needed. Gynecological problems are often treated with liver tonics (such as Dang Gui), and with herbs that are specifics to nourish the blood.

In ayurveda menstrual activity is linked to the humors: women with dominant vata are likely to have scant bleeding but severe menstrual cramps; pitta types have a heavy flow with skin rashes and anger; if kapha is dominant, the period may be over-long with nausea and breast swelling.

EMOTIONAL FACTORS
Emotional considerations may be important in treating menstrual problems: some women find menstruation or sexual intercourse distasteful, and this can lead not only to period pain and premenstrual syndrome (PMS), but to frigidity and infertility. Being comfortable with your body and its activities is an important first step in healing.

ALCHEMILLA XANTHOCHLORA   Lady's-mantle

PARTS USED *aerial parts, leaves* TASTE *astringent, slightly bitter* CHARACTER *cold, dry* MERIDIANS *liver, spleen, urinary bladder* ACTIONS *astringent, menstrual regulator, digestive tonic, anti-inflammatory, wound healer*

USES Lady's-mantle is rich in tannins, so it makes a good astringent, useful for diarrhea, sore throats, skin sores, and dermatitis. It has a gynecological action and acts as a menstrual regulator, so it is especially suitable for heavy, irregular periods related to excess heat or *pitta*. Its cool, dry nature also makes it good for a variety of heat conditions, including chronic pelvic inflammations, mouth, gum, and eye inflammations (including conjunctivitis), cystitis, and liver-fire problems. It is also used in ointments for vaginal itching.

CAUTIONS Avoid in pregnancy as it is a uterine stimulant.

ANGELICA POLYPHORMA VAR. SINENSIS   Chinese angelica/*Dang Gui*

PARTS USED *root* TASTE *sweet, pungent* CHARACTER *warm* MERIDIANS *liver, heart, spleen* ACTIONS *antibacterial, analgesic, anti-inflammatory, circulatory stimulant, reduces blood-cholesterol levels, liver tonic, sedative, uterine stimulant, rich in folic acid and vitamin B_{12}*

USES *Dang Gui* is one of the most popular Chinese tonic herbs in the West. The bottom tip of the root is said to move blood most strongly, while the uppermost part or "head" nourishes blood, invigorates the circulation, and is an important gynecological tonic, ideal for deficient blood syndromes leading to menstrual irregularities. It is very helpful in anemia and to relieve the pain of "stagnant blood." It is also laxative and helpful for constipation in the elderly.

CAUTIONS Avoid in pregnancy, diarrhea, or abdominal fullness.

CYPERUS ROTUNDUS Nutgrass/*Xiang Fu*

PARTS USED *tuber* **TASTE** *pungent, slightly bitter*
CHARACTER *neutral* **MERIDIANS** *liver, stomach*
ACTIONS *analgesic, antibacterial, antispasmodic for the uterus*

USES *Xiang Fu* encourages the circulation of *Qi*,
smooths liver *Qi* flow, and eases menstrual pains and
abnormal uterine bleeding. It is used for various
digestive problems, including colicky and period pains,
abdominal bloating, and indigestion. It is also used,
with other herbs, as a warming remedy for both wind-
cold and internal *Qi* stagnation. *Xiang Fu* can be
prepared with vinegar to enhance its painkilling effect
or with salt to help it moisten blood and fluids.
CAUTIONS Avoid in heat syndromes associated with
"deficient *Yin*."

LIGUSTICUM WALLICHII Szechuan lovage/*Chuan Xiong*

PARTS USED *rhizome* **TASTE** *pungent* **CHARACTER** *warm*
MERIDIANS *liver, pericardium, gall bladder* **ACTIONS** *antibacterial, hypotensive, sedative, uterine stimulant*

USES *Chuan Xiong* is related both to European
lovage (largely used as a culinary herb) and to *osha*
(*L. porteri*), a popular North American herb. It has
been used in China since the fourteenth century as an
invigorating blood and *Qi* remedy for menstrual and
heart problems and is also an important headache
herb, easing pain and skin eruptions caused by wind.
It is combined with *Dang Gui, Bai Shao,* and *Shu Di
Huang* in *Si Wu Tang* or "four ingredients decoction"
for menstrual irregularities and anemia. *Chuan Xiong* is
also used in remedies for coronary disease and is said
to move the *Qi* upward.
CAUTIONS Avoid in headaches caused by "deficient
Yin" or "overexuberant liver *Yang*"; avoid in pregnancy
and menorrhagia (heavy periods).

PAEONIA SUFFRUTICOSA   Tree peony/*Mu Dan Pi*

PARTS USED *root bark* TASTE *bitter, pungent* CHARACTER *slightly cold* MERIDIANS *heart, liver, kidney* ACTIONS *antibacterial, anti-allergenic, anti-inflammatory, analgesic, hypotensive, sedative*

USES The tree peony was first listed in a twelfth-century Chinese herbal, the *Pouch of Pearls (Zhen Zhu Nang)*. It is an important herb for cooling blood and clearing heat and will also invigorate the circulation, remove blood stagnation, and "clear ascending liver fire," which may be related to problems like nosebleeds. It is an important gynecological remedy, used for menstrual problems (including period pain) linked to blood stagnation and for various internal inflammations.

CAUTIONS Avoid in pregnancy and diarrhea.

VITEX AGNUS-CASTUS   Chaste-tree

PARTS USED *berries* TASTE *pungent, bitter* CHARACTER *cool* MERIDIANS *liver, stomach* ACTIONS *pituitary stimulant, hormone regulator, reproductive tonic, increases milk production, female aphrodisiac and male anaphrodisiac*

USES Chaste-tree acts on the pituitary gland to increase the production of female sex hormones. These control ovulation and the menstrual cycle, so the herb is very helpful for gynecological problems. It is used to regulate the cycle, stabilize hormone production at the menopause, improve fertility, and encourage milk production. The pituitary gland is believed to be most active in the morning, so chaste-tree is generally taken in a single daily dose before breakfast. In Greece the berries are regarded as a potent female aphrodisiac. The Chinese use a related species *(V. rotundifolia/Man Jing Zi)* to clear superficial wind-heat.

CAUTIONS Excess may cause "formication"—a sensation of ants crawling over the skin.

OTHER HERBS THAT MAY BE HELPFUL
Atlantic yam (p.79) ● *sage (p.49)* ● *mugwort (p.112)* ● *motherwort (p.134)*
● *Nu Zhen Zi (p.121)* ● *Dang Gui (p.173)* ● *Shu Di Huang (p.53)*
● *Mu Dan Pi (p.175)* ● *aloe vera (p.63)* ● *shatavari (p.105)*

WILD YAM

Menopausal problems

**In the West the menopause is generally regarded as
a natural run-down in a woman's production of sex
hormones, marking the end of the childbearing years.**

For most women the event passes by with little more inconvenience
than occasional hot flushes and night sweats. Periods often stop suddenly,
without further problem, or gradually fade away in an irregular pattern.
For other women, however, the picture can be quite different, and they
may experience major emotional upheavals, depression, weight gain, and
heavy bleeding. Today, many of these symptoms can be treated by means
of hormone replacement therapy (HRT), which boosts estrogen levels,
although critics still have certain doubts about its long-term effects. For
some women (including those with a high risk of osteoporosis) this
can be the preferred solution, but for those who want to complete this
transitional period, herbal remedies can prove beneficial, both in relieving
the more troublesome symptoms and in helping the body adjust to new
levels of functionality.

A normally healthy lifestyle with good diet, regular exercise, a happy
and fulfilled outlook, and acceptable stress levels is obviously important.
Anyone who starts out feeling depressed, overworked, or malnourished is
unlikely to pass through the menopause without trauma. Western
herbalists generally aim to use a hormone-balancing mixture of herbs to
help ease the change, although remedies can be helpful to relieve some of
the more irritating symptoms.

Chinese medicine focuses less on hormonal imbalance and more on the natural run-down in congenital Jing—our reproductive energy—stored in the kidney. This in turn leads to a weakness in two important acupuncture channels associated with reproduction (the Ren Mai and Chong channels), and they too start to decline.

According to the Chinese five-element model (see pp.14, 16), if kidney energy is weak, then it can fail to control fire and the heart may become involved as well. These factors are used to explain the typical menopausal symptoms of night sweats, hot flushes (usually affecting the upper torso and face), palpitations, emotional upsets, and tiredness. Erratic menstruation also affects blood and the liver, leading to additional weaknesses and deficiencies in these areas. Treatment usually includes herbs to tonify Qi and blood, with the emphasis being placed on the liver and kidney meridians.

In ayurveda the menopause—like other conditions that are associated with aging—is considered to be a vata problem, so treatment usually focuses on anti-vata diets and on tonifying herbs for the female reproductive organs. The upheaval in humoral balance as the body moves to a vata stage can lead to excess pitta—the cause of frequent hot flushes or short temper—as well as resulting in kapha problems, which are associated with weight gain, sleeplessness, and lethargy. Tonic remedies, notably aloe vera, chyavan prash, and shatavari, are among the most important ayurvedic treatments.

A BALANCED DIET

CHAMAELIRIUM LUTEUM

PARTS USED *root* TASTE *bitter, astringent* CHARACTER *cool, dry* MERIDIAN *liver, spleen, kidney* ACTIONS *uterine and ovarian tonic, menstrual stimulant, diuretic, estrogenic, bitter*

USES Helonias was used by Native tribes in Arkansas for treating ulcers, diarrhea, and urinary problems. It is also a tonic for the female reproductive organs and is used mainly in the West for gynecological disorders, including ovarian cysts and menopausal problems. It is stimulating for scanty or absent menstrual flow, but also helpful for excessive menstrual bleeding and spotting. It can be effective in infertility and is a good hormonal remedy for estrogen and progesterone deficiency.

CAUTIONS Avoid in pregnancy unless under professional guidance; high doses (more than 2g) may cause nausea.

CIMICIFUGA SPP. Snakeroot/*Sheng Ma*

PARTS USED *rhizome* TASTE *bitter, pungent* CHARACTER *cool, dry* MERIDIANS *lung, heart, kidney* ACTIONS *antispasmodic, anti-arthritic, anti-inflammatory, antirheumatic, mild analgesic, relaxing nervine, sedative, relaxes blood vessels, promotes menstruation, diuretic, antitussive, hypotensive, hypoglycemic*

USES Snakeroot *(C. racemosa)* is another traditional North American herb, widely used for rheumatism, yellow fever, snakebite, and gynecological problems. Recent studies have confirmed that it relieves menopausal symptoms and is strongly estrogenic. It can also be helpful for breast discomfort associated with PMS. Snakeroot is recommended for cramps, sciatica, back pain, facial neuralgia, and aches after strenuous exercise. In China *Sheng Ma (C. foetida)* is used for colds (due to wind-heat), measles, mouth ulcers, gum disease, and prolapse of the uterus.

CAUTIONS Excess may cause nausea and vomiting; avoid in pregnancy.

POLYGONUM MULTIFLORUM   Fleeceflower/*He Shou Wu*

PARTS USED *root*   TASTE *sweet, bitter, astringent*
CHARACTER *slightly warm*   MERIDIANS *liver, kidney*
ACTIONS *antibacterial, cardiotonic, hormonal action, hyperglycemic, laxative, liver stimulant, reduces cholesterol levels*

USES *He Shou Wu* (also known in the West as *Fo Ti*) is a nourishing blood tonic that is used to replenish liver and kidney *Jing*. The plant clears exterior wind and is a lubricating laxative. It is useful at the menopause to tonify the liver and kidney, but can help deficiencies here at any age. It is effective for constipation in the elderly and is used with herbs such as *Ren Shen* and *Dang Gui* for chronic debility. Fleeceflower stems *(Ye Jiao Teng)* are a heart and liver tonic.

CAUTIONS Avoid in diarrhea associated with phlegm or "deficient spleen."

TRIFOLIUM PRATENSE   Red clover

PARTS USED *flowers*   TASTE *sweet, bland*   CHARACTER *cool*
MERIDIANS *lung, kidney, urinary bladder*   ACTIONS *cleansing, antispasmodic, diuretic, expectorant, sedative, possible estrogenic activity, reputedly anticancerous*

USES Red clover is a cleansing remedy for gout and skin problems, such as psoriasis and childhood eczema, and an effective treatment for bronchitis and whooping cough. In the 1930s the flowers were used for breast, ovarian, and lymphatic cancers, but more recent interest has focused on its estrogenic activity. It is an effective menopausal remedy and seems to offer natural hormone replacement, although detailed research is still limited. Externally an infusion of the flowers can be used as a wash for wounds, persistent sores, eye inflammations, and insect bites.

CAUTIONS Possible contraceptive effect, so it should be avoided by women trying to conceive.

OTHER HERBS THAT MAY BE HELPFUL
gokshura (p.168) ● Dang Gui (p.173) ● asafetida (p.95) ● ashwagandha
(p.107) ● damiana (p.171) ● Shu Di Huang (p.53) ● fenugreek (p.81)
● ginseng (p.106) ● lotus (p.80) ● rose (p.113) ● shatavari (p.105)

ROSE PETALS

Aphrodisiacs

Stress, overwork, alcohol, and excess caffeine can all contribute to low

libido and impotence. For many men, doubts about their performance are

enough to prevent satisfactory erection and orgasm, while for many

women tension and stress can lead to muscle constriction, making

intercourse painful. The rhythm of the menstrual cycle also plays its part

in women's libido, which often tends to rise in mid-cycle. At other times it

can be quite natural to feel less like sexual intercourse and partners

should respect this natural rhythm. Worry over infertility (see box) adds

further stress, but herbs can help improve general health and readiness

for conception, as well as stimulate sperm production, although much also

depends on lifestyle and the mental attitude of both partners.

In TCM reproductive energies are stored in the kidneys, so warming

kidney tonics are often used for infertility and impotence. Indian tantric

THE STRUGGLE TO CONCEIVE

For many couples the struggle to conceive becomes an all-consuming preoccupation, simply adding to the tensions. Male infertility is generally associated with a low sperm count, and recent studies suggest that too much junk food and contaminants in the form of pesticides can contribute to the problem.

tradition and ayurveda lay great emphasis on strengthening sexual energy, but this is associated with creative energy and general vitality as well. Aphrodisiac remedies are known as vajikarana (from "vaji," a stallion)— their focus on reproductive energy helps to energize all the body's tissues (dhatus). By increasing sexual energy, the vajikarana help to renew our lives.

CROCUS SATIVUS Saffron/*Fan Hong Hua*/*nagakeshara*

PARTS USED *flower stigma* TASTE *sweet, pungent*
CHARACTER *neutral* MERIDIANS *heart, liver*
ACTIONS *aphrodisiac, rejuvenative, promotes menstruation, carminative, antispasmodic, stimulating*

USES Traditionally used in India as a blood tonic, stimulant, and aphrodisiac, saffron is very restorative and in ayurveda is used to strengthen feelings of compassion. It is one of the best anti-*pitta* remedies and a potent aphrodisiac, especially for women. It helps to enhance other tonic herbs, so it is often added to other remedies. In China it is seen as invigorating for the blood circulation and clears blood stagnation and stagnant liver *Qi*. It is used for menstrual problems and as a post-partum tonic. It is used with *shatavari* or *Dang Gui* as a tonic for the female reproductive organs.

CAUTIONS Avoid in pregnancy.

SCHISANDRA CHINENSIS Chinese magnolia-vine/*Wu Wei Zi*

PARTS USED *fruit* TASTE *sour* CHARACTER *warm*
MERIDIANS *lung, heart, kidney* ACTIONS *antibacterial, astringent, aphrodisiac, circulatory stimulant, digestive stimulant, expectorant, hypotensive, sedative, tonic, uterine stimulant*

USES Although the taste of *Wu Wei Zi* is generally given as "sour," the name actually means "five taste seeds" and it was once regarded as combining all five classic Chinese tastes. The herb is used to replenish *Qi* (especially lung *Qi*), tonify the kidney and heart, calm the spirit *(Shen)*, and strengthen body fluids—it has also been regarded as an aphrodisiac for at least 2,000 years. It can be taken for coughs, skin rashes, chronic diarrhea, insomnia, and severe shock; with *Bu Gu Zhi* in kidney deficiency; and with *Huang Qi* for deficient *Yang*. Its five tastes reputedly help all five *Zang* organs.

CAUTIONS Avoid in internal heat or superficial syndromes.

OTHER HERBS THAT MAY BE HELPFUL
camomile (p.192) ● *lemon-balm (p.111)* ● *Chen Pi (p.41)*
● *curly dock (p.151)*

DRIED CAMOMILE

Pregnancy

Herbal remedies have been used by generations of

women to ease the problems associated with pregnancy

and childbirth. Many provide a safe alternative to orthodox remedies,

but a great many also need to be avoided as they are potentially

damaging to the fetus. All medication—including herbs—should be

avoided in the first three months of pregnancy and any treatments should

be taken for as short a time as possible.

Fortunately most ailments in pregnancy are minor and self-limiting,

although they can be troublesome—as with morning sickness. In Western

tradition this is treated with anti-emetic herbs, such as camomile and

ginger. In China, however, the cause of the morning sickness must first be

identified—upward flaring of liver Qi, perhaps, to be treated with

remedies including Dang Gui (usually avoided in pregnancy in the West)

and ginseng; or spleen and stomach deficiency, when mixtures containing

Chen Pi, Huang Qin, and Fu Ling would be prescribed.

GINGER

Swollen ankles or edema causing puffiness to the head

and face can be another common problem. Western

medicine explains this in terms of changes in the concentration

of proteins in the blood, making it easier for fluids to leak from

blood vessels to surrounding tissues. Chinese theory

explains it in terms of excess dampness caused by

spleen or kidney deficiency, related to an

imbalance in normal Qi flows due to the growing

fetus. Remedies focus on invigorating spleen energies with herbs like ginseng or Bai Zhu, while clearing the dampness with ginger or Fu Ling.

Chinese medicine also ascribes many of the familiar minor ills of pregnancy, such as low backache, abdominal discomfort, or an occasional show of blood, to a "restless fetus." According to TCM, a healthy, trouble-free pregnancy needs an abundance of Qi and Xue, which will maintain the balance between Yin and Yang. If Qi is weak, or there are problems with the smooth circulation of blood, then fetal growth is disrupted and "restlessness" follows. Again, differential diagnosis is important: if pain in the lower back and legs predominates, then it could be kidney deficiency; if there is more vaginal bleeding and abdominal distention, then it could be a liver problem; while swollen ankles and nausea beyond the third month may indicate a problem with cold.

APPLES

Apart from its physical discomforts, pregnancy is also a time of enhanced spiritual awareness, when women feel highly creative and greatly in tune with the wider nature of their being—a time when ayurveda suggests some of its more potent tonics, such as shatavari, ashwagandha, or bala, to help build this inner strength.

HERBS TO AVOID IN PREGNANCY

Avoid the following herbs completely during pregnancy: barberry, basil oil, blue cohosh, camomile oil, Dang Gui, feverfew, golden seal, lady's-mantle, motherwort, mugwort, myrrh, snakeroot, and wormwood.

Avoid regular large or high doses of: Atlantic yam, betony, celery seed, Chen Pi, cinnamon, elder bark, fennel, fenugreek, ginseng, lavender, nutmeg, parsley, rhubarb root, sage, tabasco pepper, thyme, vervain, and yarrow; culinary use is safe.

EQUISETUM ARVENSE   Horse-tail

PARTS USED *aerial parts, juice* **TASTE** *bitter, astringent*
CHARACTER *cold, dry* **MERIDIANS** *liver, urinary bladder,
lung* **ACTIONS** *astringent, styptic, diuretic, anti-inflammatory,
tissue healer*

USES Horse-tail grew in prehistoric times and its
decayed remains now form much of the world's coal
seams. The plant is rich in silica, which is very healing,
and has been used largely for urinary-tract problems,
including cystitis—common in pregnancy—and prostate
disorders. It can also be helpful in deep-seated lung
problems, including chronic bronchitis. It is cool and
dry, so clears damp-heat problems and can be helpful
in inflammatory conditions, including eye inflammations
and digestive disorders.

CAUTIONS Take additional B vitamins if using horse-tail
for any length of time, as it can encourage breakdown
of these vitamins in digestion.

FILIPENDULA ULMARIA   Meadowsweet

PARTS USED *aerial parts, leaves* **TASTE** *astringent*
CHARACTER *cold, moist* **MERIDIANS** *stomach, kidney, urinary
bladder* **ACTIONS** *anti-inflammatory, antirheumatic, soothing
digestive remedy, diuretic, diaphoretic, antacid, astringent*

USES Meadowsweet's old botanical name, *Spiraea
ulmaria*, gave its name to the drug "aspirin," which
was patented in 1899: the herb was an original
source of salicylate compounds. Meadowsweet is used
internally for gastritis, indigestion, and heartburn, as
well as for easing arthritic and rheumatic aches and
pains. It is ideal for the heartburn and indigestion
common in pregnancy and can ease the symptoms of
morning sickness. It is also useful in arthritis and gout to
clear accumulated toxins and increase urination.

CAUTIONS Best avoided by those sensitive to salicylates.

RUBUS SPP. Raspberry/*Fu Pen Zi*

PARTS USED *leaves, fruit* TASTE *sweet, sour* CHARACTER *cool*
MERIDIANS *stomach, kidney* ACTIONS *astringent, partus
praeparator, astringent, stimulant, digestive remedy, tonic,
diuretic, laxative*

USES In the West raspberry leaf *(R. idaeus)* is best
known for its tonifying effect on the uterus and as a
preparative for childbirth. It is generally taken for six to
eight weeks before the confinement and during labor to
help strengthen the womb. It is also used as a gargle
for sore throats, in eyebaths for inflammations, and may
be taken for diarrhea and period pain. The Chinese
raspberry *(R. chingii)* is regarded as a tonic for the liver
and kidney and is used mainly for urinary disorders.
It is believed to improve vision, combat early graying of
the hair, and be effective for impotence and infertility.
CAUTIONS Avoid during the first six months of
pregnancy; avoid *Fu Pen Zi* if urination is difficult.

ZINGIBER OFFICINALE Ginger/*Jiang/adraka*

PARTS USED *root* TASTE *pungent* CHARACTER *warm*
MERIDIANS *lung, spleen, stomach* ACTIONS *anti-emetic,
antispasmodic, antiseptic, carminative, circulatory stimulant,
diaphoretic, expectorant, peripheral vasodilator, topically
rubefacient*

USES Ginger helps to combat the nausea and vomiting
of morning and motion sickness. It is warming in chills
and carminative, easing flatulence and indigestion. The
Chinese use fresh ginger *(Sheng Jiang)*, a warming
remedy for wind-cold chills, to strengthen *Wei Qi* and
warm the middle *Jiao*. Dried ginger *(Gan Jiang)* has a
more tonic action, helping to replenish *Yang* and warm
spleen and stomach. The peel of fresh ginger root *(Sheng
Jiang Pi)* is diuretic. In ayurveda ginger is taken with honey
to reduce *kapha* and with salt to treat *vata* syndromes.
CAUTIONS Avoid in internal heat syndromes.

RASPBERRY LEAF

Childbirth

Modern Western medicine has tended to make childbirth a suitably high-tech affair, with constant monitoring of the fetus, heavy dependence on pain-killing drugs, and a fondness for Cesarean sections at every opportunity. Many women, too, believe that to "do their best for the baby" they must submit to whatever modern medicine demands of them.

For generations herbal remedies were all that women had to sustain them during a difficult labor or problematic birth. Given the high risk of death in childbirth endured by our great-grandmothers, no one would urge a return to such limited resources, but the herbs used are still effective and can help during the early stages of labor and in the post-natal period. During labor herbal infusions can help to calm the nerves, stimulate the womb, and encourage regular contractions. Teas of betony (p.121), rose petals, Atlantic yam (p.79), and raspberry leaves (p.185) can help, with hot compresses soaked in marigold, mugwort, or betony infusion applied to the lower abdomen. After the birth, take homeopathic arnica every 15 minutes for several hours, while a Chinese practice for the new mother is to eat plenty of **Dang Gui** *and lamb stew in the weeks following the birth.*

PARTUS PRAEPARATORS

These preparations for childbirth were traditionally taken in the last six to eight weeks of pregnancy to prepare the womb for labor: in Europe raspberry leaf, lady's-mantle, motherwort, and St.-John's-wort were all used in this way, as were blue cohosh, snakeroot, and helonias in North America.

CAULOPHYLLUM THALICTROIDES Blue cohosh

PARTS USED *root, rhizome* TASTE *bitter, pungent*
CHARACTER *warm, dry* MERIDIANS *lung, kidney*
ACTIONS *anti-inflammatory, antispasmodic, uterine
stimulant, diuretic, menstrual stimulant, antirheumatic,
diaphoretic, uterine tonic*

USES Known as squaw root in North America because
of its traditional role in treating various gynecological
problems, blue cohosh is still used largely as a
menstrual regulator and to ease uterine and ovarian
pain. The herb is highly restorative for the womb and
helps to encourage contractions in labor. It is a useful
herb for menopausal problems, combating estrogen
deficiency, and is helpful for PMS and period pain.
It is also a cleansing remedy for rheumatism, gout,
and arthritis, helping to clear excess urates.
CAUTIONS Avoid in pregnancy, except during labor,
as it is a uterine stimulant.

PULSATILLA VULGARIS Pasque-flower

PARTS USED *aerial parts* TASTE *bitter, pungent*
CHARACTER *warm, dry* MERIDIANS *heart, lung, urinary
bladder* ACTIONS *nerve relaxant, sedative, alterative,
antibacterial, analgesic, antispasmodic*

USES Pasque-flower is ideal for pain or inflammation
involving the reproductive organs—especially the
ovaries, testicles, and prostate gland—and is sedative
and soothing for PMS, painful menstruation, and
menopausal hot flushes. The herb helps to ease anxiety
and fear, so it can be helpful if the mother is nervous in
labor; it is also good for insomnia, headaches, and
depression. It can be used to reduce inflammation in
eye disorders, for glaucoma, and to improve eyesight.
CAUTIONS The fresh herb contains an irritant, antibacterial substance; however, this is destroyed on
drying and the plant can then safely be used.

Herbal birthing kit

Planning a herbal birthing kit will depend very much on the approach of your doctor and maternity hospital: if they have a positive approach to herbal medicine and are supportive, then remedies may be used throughout labor and in the immediate post-delivery period. If not, herbal remedies will be confined to home use. Prepare the following mixtures well before they are likely to be needed:

For home use in the early stages

• Around 4oz/100g of a mixture containing equal amounts of betony, rose petals, and raspberry leaves ready to make into infusions (2tsp per cup); alternatively, use 4tsp/20ml of tincture of each of these herbs with an equal amount of water and store in dropper bottles.

• 10 drops each of lavender and jasmine oil in 2fl oz/50ml of almond oil in a small bottle for home massage before heading into hospital.

To take into hospital

• A bottle containing 10 drops of sage oil in 2fl oz/50ml of almond oil for abdominal massage as labor progresses.

• A vacuum flask containing warm betony, rose petal, and mugwort infusion with 2–3 cloves added, to help increase contractions during the later stages.

• A vacuum flask containing equal amounts of dried basil and motherwort infusion to take immediately after the birth to help clear the placenta.

• Arnica 30X tablets to take every 15–20 minutes after the birth for a few hours to speed recovery.

• A small bottle of infused marigold oil with 5–10 drops of lavender oil added to help perineal damage (see below).

To have ready at home on your return

• 4oz/100g dried marigold or camomile flowers to use in infusions for compresses and washes for perineal damage.

• Raspberry leaf and ginger tincture for treating after-pains.

• Marigold cream for use on sore nipples.

• 4oz/100g of lemon-balm or St.-John's-wort in case of post-natal depression.

BABIES AND CHILDREN

When to seek help for sick children

If your child's symptoms include any of the following, seek urgent help:
- *Convulsions or fits*
- *Breathing problems or unusual drowsiness/lethargy*
- *An unusual, high-pitched cry in babies and toddlers*
- *Severe diarrhea or vomiting*
- *Milder diarrhea, which continues for more than 12 hours*
- *Neck stiffness with signs of fever, headache, or a rash*
- *Temperatures that rise above 102°F/39°C for more than a couple of hours.*

 ## Western Approach

One of the major problems with Western medicine's treatment of children is its overuse of antibiotics: the slightest chill sends parents in search of a pill to restore normality. Physicians are starting to realize that this overuse can weaken the developing immune system and lead not only to increased allergies but also to poor immunity to infection in later life. Most children's infections respond well to simple herbal remedies.

 ## Chinese Approach

The vast majority of children's illnesses are regarded in TCM as "superficial"—due to "evils," rather than the internal imbalances of adult conditions. Colds, minor injuries, fevers, and stomach upsets are almost always ascribed to attack by a combination of "evils." Children are also energetic and hot, and more likely to suffer from fire syndromes—hyperactivity is blamed on excess liver fire and treated with cooling herbs.

 ## Ayurvedic Approach

In ayurveda childhood is regarded as a *kapha* stage of life—water feeding new tissues and growth. *Kapha* also suggests phlegm and problems like nasal catarrh and glue ear, or excess mucus leading to lung problems. Normally these would be treated with *kapha*-reducing spices, but children need a balanced mix of all six tastes for healthy growth, so they are generally given milk boiled with a little cinnamon, ginger, cloves, or cardamom instead.

OTHER HERBS THAT MAY BE HELPFUL
marigold (p.63) ● *cloves (p.156)* ● *St.-John's-wort (p.111)* ● *horse-tail p.184)* ● *comfrey (p.147)* ● *tea tree (p.195)* ● *fennel (p.65)*

Babies' ailments

Small babies are demanding, noisy, and disruptive—
no household is ever quite the same once one
arrives and, for many months, life revolves
around this little individual. Everyday problems include colic, sleeplessness,
and the occasional rash. Rushed or tense feed times are often the cause of
gut spasms and colic, so maintaining a relaxed, peaceful environment is
important. Young babies will often quite happily accept herbal teas by
bottle, if they are started early enough. Recent studies have even shown
that babies will happily eat quite bitter-tasting vegetables at a young age
and introducing these foods early on may prevent feeding problems later.

Problems such as cradle cap (see p.193) and diaper rash are common.
Diaper rash may be caused by irregular or inefficient changes or may be
related to digestive imbalance and yeast infections.
Teething is not usually a problem before four months,
although it can start at a few weeks, adding to the
stresses of coping with a new baby. Herbal lotions
containing one or two drops of camomile and sage oil
make a useful gum rub to ease discomfort. A traditional
Chinese remedy is to put one drop of clove oil in a teaspoon of
almond oil and gently massage the baby's lower back.

Sleepless babies soon make the rest of the household tense, which
simply compounds the stress and leads to frayed tempers. Making sure
that the baby's room is not too hot is important—as are plenty of cuddles.

FEEDING BOTTLE

In China many everyday problems with babies are treated using finger massage: a traditional treatment for sleeplessness is to stroke the forearms slowly in one direction for 100 strokes, using a little very dilute camomile oil (one drop in 4tsp/20ml sweet almond oil) on your finger.

Similar massage can also be used for colic: massage the baby's lower spine, stroking from the lumbar region to the coccyx up to 200 times in one direction (likewise for constipation). If the baby is suffering from diarrhea, then the motion should be from the coccyx to the lumbar area.

Breastfeeding is acknowledged as the preferred option for babies—an ideal food, breast milk helps to strengthen the immune system with no risk of allergies developing, as may happen with cow's milk derivatives and artificial substitutes. Breastfeeding is also an ideal way to pass on herbs to young babies: the mother simply needs to drink a suitable tea—camomile for sleeplessness, agrimony for diarrhea—before feeds to enable a dilute amount of the remedy to reach the baby via the breast milk.

TEASPOON OF OIL

DOSES FOR BABIES AND CHILDREN

Children's dosages vary, depending on the age and body weight of the child. Seek professional advice before giving any herb internally to very young babies, apart from those suggestions given for bottle-fed infusions. Otherwise, follow the recommendations given below:

- *For children aged six months to one year, give one-tenth of the adult dose*

- *For children aged one to two years, give one-fifth of the adult dose*

- *By the age of three to four years, gradually increase to one-quarter of the adult dose*

- *By the age of six to seven years, give one-third of the adult dose*

- *By the age of nine to ten years, give half the adult dose*

- *By puberty, you can give the full adult dose*

Agrimony/*Xian He Cao*

PARTS USED *aerial parts/leaves* TASTE *bitter, astringent*
CHARACTER *neutral* MERIDIANS *lung, spleen, liver*
ACTIONS *astringent, diuretic, tissue healer, stops bleeding,
stimulates bile flow, some antiviral activity*

USES European agrimony *(A. eupatoria)* is an astringent,
bitter herb with a long tradition as a wound healer. It is
diuretic and contains silica, which makes it a good
healing remedy for urinary disorders. It is ideal for
diarrhea, especially in children, and can be taken by
nursing mothers to ease diarrhea in small babies. It is
helpful in cases of food intolerance, strengthening and
repairing the gut. The oriental species *(A. pilosa)* is
used in similar ways in China to stop bleeding
(including nosebleeds) and combat toxic infections.
CAUTIONS Avoid *Xian He Cao* in pathogenic heat and
excess fire syndromes.

Roman camomile
German camomile

PARTS USED *flowers* TASTE *bitter, sweet* CHARACTER *warm,
moist* MERIDIANS *pericardium, lung, spleen, liver, large
intestine* ACTIONS *anti-inflammatory, antispasmodic, bitter,
sedative, carminative, anti-emetic, anti-allergenic*

USES Both herbs make a calming tea to combat stress,
anxiety, and insomnia and can also ease indigestion
and gastrointestinal spasms, nausea, poor appetite,
nasal catarrh, and candidiasis. Camomile is ideal for
children and is often given to calm hyperactivity, travel
sickness, digestive upsets, and threadworms, while
homeopathic remedies are recommended for teething
and colic in babies. The infusion can also be used in
eye baths for conjunctivitis or as an effective wash for
skin rashes.
CAUTIONS The fresh plant may cause contact dermatitis.

TILIA CORDATA Linden

PARTS USED *flowers* TASTE *pungent, sweet, astringent*
CHARACTER *warm, dry* MERIDIANS *lung, liver*
ACTIONS *antispasmodic, diaphoretic, diuretic, sedative,*
anticoagulant, immune stimulant, digestive remedy

USES Linden flowers are a popular after-dinner tisane in
France, taken to encourage relaxation and improve
digestion. The plant is calming for the nerves and can
help reduce high blood pressure, ease migraines,
tension headaches, and symptoms associated with
heart *Qi* constraint. It is believed to combat the build-up
of fatty deposits in the blood vessels that can lead to
atherosclerosis and is diaphoretic, being used to lower
body temperature in fevers. As an astringent, it can
also ease nosebleeds and soothe the bowel in diarrhea
and childhood tummy upsets.

CAUTIONS None noted.

VIOLA TRICOLOR Johnny-jump-up

PARTS USED *aerial parts* TASTE *pungent, sweet*
CHARACTER *neutral* MERIDIANS *kidney, urinary bladder*
ACTIONS *expectorant, anti-inflammatory, diuretic, anti-*
rheumatic, laxative, stabilizes capillary membranes

USES Heartsease, or wild pansy, is good for coughs,
bronchitis, and whooping cough,and can soothe skin
inflammations, acne, nettle rash, and eczema. It is rich
in flavonoids (including rutin), so it will strengthen
capillary walls. Heartsease infusion can be used as a
wash to bathe skin sores, diaper rash, and cradle cap
(a scaly dermatitis affecting the scalps of newborn
babies, which may be due to overactive sweat glands
—it is not serious or contagious, but does look
unsightly). The herb also makes a good wound healer
and is relaxing for the nerves when taken internally.

CAUTIONS None noted.

OTHER HERBS THAT MAY BE HELPFUL
neem (p.67) ● thyme (p.43) ● echinacea (p.45)
● lemon-balm (p.111) ● hyssop (p.42) ● mulberry (p.198)
● marigold (p.63) ● camomile (p.192) ● marshmallow (p.78)

ELDERFLOWER

Infections and infestations

Childhood infections are usually fairly minor and

respond well to simple home remedies—but complications can

occur and sometimes (as in measles) professional help is essential. Most of

the problems are caused by viruses, so antibiotics will have no effect and

herbal remedies to strengthen the immune system may therefore be ideal.

Chinese medicine treats most such infections as superficial syndromes

caused by "external evils," so the sorts of remedies used for common

colds (see p.44) are generally preferred. Ayurveda similarly regards these

sorts of problems as mostly excess pitta problems (causing fevers).

Herbs may be used for many of the common infections of childhood.

Chicken pox (varicella), for example, can be treated by strengthening the

immune system with echinacea or Huang Qi and thus easing the

symptoms. A lotion made from equal amounts of marigold infusion and

distilled witch hazel can be used on the irritant skin rash. Measles will

respond to herbs for feverish chills, with hyssop or marshmallow leaf

being used to ease coughs, and eyebright (p.65), self-heal (p.199), or

elderflowers (p.55) in eyebaths to soothe painful eyes.

Children are also likely to suffer from infestations of lice and nits (eggs),

outbreaks of which are commonplace in schools. The problem is often

treated with powerful insecticidal shampoos that have unpleasant side

effects; a gentler alternative is to use tea-tree or thyme oils, or neem

infusions, in scalp massage or added to the hair rinse after shampooing.

For the appropriate dosages for children, see p.191.

Boneset

PARTS USED *aerial parts* **TASTE** *bitter, pungent, astringent*
CHARACTER *cold, dry* **MERIDIANS** *lung, liver, spleen*
ACTIONS *immune stimulant, diaphoretic, peripheral vasodilator, laxative, stimulates bile flow*

USES Boneset is so called from its traditional use in North America as a remedy for flu-type fevers with their associated aches and pains. Settlers soon adopted the herb as a cure-all and it reached Europe in the nineteenth century. The plant is ideal for the early stages of feverish colds (especially wind-heat types), and can be helpful to control the coughing in measles. It is also a good cleansing remedy for the liver and cooling for liver fire. It is a useful plant in debility and convalescence, helping to stimulate the appetite, clear lingering coughs, and strengthen the immune system.
CAUTIONS None noted.

Tea tree

PARTS USED *essential oil* **TASTE** *pungent, bitter*
CHARACTER *hot, dry* **MERIDIANS** *lung, large intestine, spleen* **ACTIONS** *antiseptic, antibacterial, antifungal, antiviral, immune stimulant, antiparasitic*

USES European interest in the Australian tea tree dates back to the 1920s, when the strong antibacterial action of its oil was first investigated in France. Recently a thriving tea-tree industry has grown up, which has led to a number of highly adulterated oils appearing. True tea-tree oil is one of the few that does not usually irritate the mucous membranes and can be used neat on the skin. It is a very effective antimicrobial, useful in washes for wounds or fungal infections, in chest rubs for feverish colds, and for *Staphylococcus aureus* infections. The oil is good for clearing nits and lice.
CAUTIONS None noted.

OTHER HERBS THAT MAY BE HELPFUL
marigold (p.63) ● camomile (p.192) ● agrimony (p.192)

Other childhood ailments

DRIED MARIGOLD

Children suffer from constipation and stomach upsets, headaches and sore throats, sleeplessness, and urinary infections just as their parents do, and herbal remedies can prove just as helpful, although lower doses are needed (see box on p.191).

*Childhood is also the time when allergies are most troublesome, with eczema and asthma being commonplace. In many cases overprocessed foods are to blame: in ayurveda raw milk is always boiled with spices for children in order to reduce its **kapha-forming effect**. In the West children drink precooked, devitalized, pasteurized milk, which is far more mucus-forming, so it is hardly surprising that problems such as glue ear or secretory otitis media (which is typified by recurrent ear infections, earache, progressive hearing loss, and copious sticky secretions from the ear) occur as a result.*

Food intolerance is also frequently blamed in the West for hyperactivity, sleeplessness, and poor concentration in children. In Chinese theory liver-fire syndromes are blamed for such conditions, but the problem is likely to be exacerbated by pollutants clogging up the liver, so giving children natural food products—organic if at all possible—rather than synthetic "junk" products is always a sound idea.

BILIOUS ATTACKS

Bilious attacks can be a problem with some children: these may be related to migraine in later life and are often associated with food intolerance, so careful monitoring of the diet at this stage may help to prevent problems later on in life.

California-poppy

ESCHSCHOLZIA CALIFORNICA

PARTS USED *aerial parts* TASTE *sour* CHARACTER *neutral*
MERIDIANS *lung, large intestine* ACTIONS *sedative, nerve relaxant, anodyne, mild hypnotic*

USES Although a member of the poppy family, California-poppy—also known as nightcap—is only a mild soporific and can even be suitable for sleepless children. It is a useful pain-killer and may be helpful in stress or for digestive upsets and bowel problems associated with nervous tension. It combines well with passion-flower for hyperactivity in small children or with lavender flowers as an night-time tea for insomnia. The plant is easy to grow in the garden as an annual and can be used either fresh or dried.
CAUTIONS None noted.

Eucalyptus

EUCALYPTUS GLOBULUS

PARTS USED *essential oil* TASTE *pungent, bitter*
CHARACTER *cool* MERIDIANS *lung, large intestine, urinary bladder* ACTIONS *antiseptic, antiviral, antifungal, antispasmodic, stimulant, reduces fever, hypoglycemic*

USES Originally an Aboriginal remedy, eucalyptus arrived in Europe in the nineteenth century and has been used as a potent antiseptic for infections ever since. It is helpful for superficial syndromes associated with wind-heat and is ideal in measles and chicken pox, as well as in acute rheumatism and headaches. The oil is generally used in steam inhalations or directly as an inhalant by putting a few drops of the neat oil on a handkerchief; or it can be diluted in almond oil and used as a chest rub or massage for aching muscles and joints; two to five drops of the oil can be taken internally by adults for the same purposes with a spoon of honey. Fresh leaves can be used in inhalants and washes.
CAUTIONS None noted.

MORUS SPP. Mulberry/*Sang*

PARTS USED *leaves, root bark, twigs, fruits* TASTE *sweet, bitter* CHARACTER *cold* MERIDIANS *lung, liver* ACTIONS *various parts of the mulberry have been found to be analgesic, anti-asthmatic, antibacterial, antitussive, diaphoretic, diuretic, expectorant, hypotensive, hypoglycemic, and sedative*

USES The white mulberry *(M. alba)* is one of China's most versatile medicinal trees. The leaves *(Sang Ye)* are included in remedies for feverish colds, while the root bark *(Sang Bai Pi)* is a good cough remedy for hot conditions and asthma. Both are gentle—ideal for infections and seasonal chills in children and toddlers. The twigs *(Sang Zhi)* are used for rheumatic pains, and the fruit spikes *(Sang Shen)* as a *Yin* tonic to nourish the blood and combat anemia. Black mulberry *(M. nigra)* leaves are now known to help in diabetes.

CAUTIONS Avoid *Sang Bai Pi* and *Sang Ye* in cold conditions and *Sang Shen* in diarrhea.

NEPETA CATARIA Catmint

PARTS USED *aerial parts* TASTE *pungent, bitter* CHARACTER *cool, dry* MERIDIANS *large intestine, kidney* ACTIONS *antispasmodic, diaphoretic, carminative, gentle nerve relaxant, antidiarrheal, increases menstrual flow*

USES As the name suggests, catmint is a favorite plant of cats. It is a gentle herb, ideal for children and suitable for colic, feverish chills, and hyperactivity. It is useful for colds associated with wind-heat and characterized by headaches, chills, fevers, and sore throats; it also makes a cooling wash for skin irritations, as in chicken pox or measles. It is helpful in gastritis and menstrual cramps and, like other members of the mint family, will ease the symptoms of indigestion although it does not contain any irritant menthol.

CAUTIONS Avoid in pregnancy.

PRUNELLA VULGARIS Self-heal/*Xia Ku Cao*

PARTS USED *flower spike* **TASTE** *bitter, pungent* **CHARACTER** *cool* **MERIDIANS** *lung, gall bladder* **ACTIONS** *antibacterial, hypotensive, diuretic, astringent, wound healer*

USES Self-heal is a common European wild flower, traditionally used in folk medicine as a wound healer— hence its English name. The Chinese view it as an important cooling remedy for the liver and it can be very effective in calming hyperactive children, who are often suffering from "liver-fire syndromes," which may also be associated with eye inflammations, headaches, vertigo, and irritability. *Xia Ku Cao* is often combined with *Ju Hua* or *Xiang Fu* for liver problems. It will clear swellings in conditions such as mastitis, mumps, goiter, and lymphatic disorders, which are associated with constrained liver *Qi*.

CAUTIONS Avoid if the spleen or stomach is weak.

ZEA MAYS Cornsilk/*Yu Mi Xu*

PARTS USED *stigma* **TASTE** *sweet* **CHARACTER** *neutral* **MERIDIANS** *liver, gall bladder, urinary bladder* **ACTIONS** *diuretic, soothing for the urinary tract, mild bile stimulant*

USES Cornsilk comprises the long, silky flower threads from maize plants, which dry to form a crinkled mass resembling red beard clippings. It is a soothing diuretic for irritant and inflamed bladder and urinary-tract disorders, including prostate problems and cystitis; it can be helpful for bedwetting in children, where this is associated with bladder irritation, and works well combined with agrimony. The plant is regarded as a diuretic in China, but is also used to stimulate bile flow, lower blood-sugar levels in diabetes, and help reduce high blood pressure.

CAUTIONS None noted.

First-aid kit

The kitchen staples and a basic assortment of

herbal remedies can deal with the vast majority of

minor, self-limiting household ills just as effectively as—and

far more economically than—pharmaceuticals from the drugstore.

Your herbal first-aid kit can include: ordinary Indian tea as a remedy

for diarrhea; honey to put on suppurating wounds in order to clear the

pus; and a piece of fresh ginger root to use for nausea and chills. It can

also extend to an Aloe vera plant on the kitchen windowsill for treating

minor burns, scalds, sunburn, and grazes—simply break off a leaf, split it

open, and apply the thick gel that oozes out to the affected area.

As well as the usual stock of bandages, cotton-wool swabs, and

sticking plasters, some store-bought herbal products to add to your

staples should include those listed here.

HERBAL REMEDY	How to use
ARNICA	cream or ointment for use on bruises and sprains (but not on broken skin because of its toxicity)
ARNICA (HOMEOPATHIC)	6X tablets to take after any shocks or accidents—let a tablet dissolve on the tongue at 30-minute intervals until the patient feels more settled
CAMOMILE FLOWERS	teabags for making quick cups of tea to treat shock, nervous upsets, insomnia, and indigestion
COMFREY	ointment or infused oil to encourage the healing of wounds and bruises and as a massage for sprains and strains
ECHINACEA	tablets or capsules as a herbal antibiotic for colds, influenza, and other infections; tablets or capsules generally each contain around 200mg of dried herb, and you can take up to 600mg per dose, three times a day

ELDERFLOWER	teabags for colds and catarrh; alternatively keep a bottle of concentrated elderflower cordial in the house, dilute with hot water, and use in the same way
FENNEL	teabags for indigestion and digestive upsets; or use the soaked bags as pads for eyestrain and inflammations
GARLIC	cloves, or capsules containing garlic oil—rub the fresh cloves on acne and pimples or use them to draw corns; take the capsules for infections or use the oil that they contain for ear problems
LAVENDER	oil ready diluted in almond oil—use 1tsp/5ml lavender oil to 4tsp/20ml almond oil and store in a smal dark-glass bottle; use as a massage medium for headaches, for dabbing on cold sores and minor burns, or add it to the bathtub for a relaxing soak
MARIGOLD	cream—an antiseptic and antifungal remedy for cuts, grazes, and fungal infections such as athlete's foot
MARSHMALLOW AND SLIPPERY-ELM	ointment for drawing stubborn splinters, boils, and insect stings and to soothe irritant skin rashes
MYRRH	tincture to add to mouthwashes and gargles for sore throats, gum problems, and mouth ulcers
PEPPERMINT	teabags, or a small bottle of peppermint emulsion, for indigestion and nausea—either make a cup of infusion or add three to four drops of the emulsion to a cup of hot water
SLIPPERY ELM	tablets to line the stomach and reduce inflammation in gastritis, indigestion, or as a preventative for hangovers
TEA TREE	oil is antiseptic and antifungal for use on cuts and grazes, warts, fungal infections, and cold sores
VERVAIN	teabags for infusions for stress and digestive problems
WITCH HAZEL (DISTILLED)	for use as a styptic on cuts and grazes and to soothe minor burns, sunburn, insect bites, varicose veins, and bruises

201

Glossary

ADRENAL CORTEX The outer part of the ductless adrenal glands, located on top of the kidneys, which produces several important hormones

ADRENAL GLAND A two-part gland located just above each kidney

ALTERATIVE A substance that improves the function of various organs—notably those involved with the breakdown and excretion of waste products—to bring about a gradual change of state; blood cleanser

AMEBICIDAL Has the power to destroy amebae

ANALGESIC Deadens pain

ANAPHRODISIAC Reduces sexual desire

ANODYNE Pain-killing

ANTACID Counters the effects of stomach acid and relieves indigestion

ANTHELMINTIC Destroys or expels worms; antiparasitic

ANTI-ALLERGENIC Reduces allergic reactions

ANTIBACTERIAL Destroys or inhibits the growth of bacteria

ANTICATARRHAL Reduces the production of mucus

ANTICOAGULANT Retards coagulation of the blood

ANTIDIARRHEAL A remedy that has the ability to stop diarrhea and soothe an irritable bowel

ANTI-ECZEMA Combats eczema

ANTI-EMETIC Allays a sense of nausea and prevents vomiting

ANTIFUNGAL Destroys or inhibits the growth of fungi

ANTIHIDROTIC Inhibits perspiration

ANTIHISTAMINIC Treats allergic conditions; counteracts the effects of histamine

ANTI-INFLAMMATORY Alleviates inflammation

ANTIMALARIAL Combats the effects of malaria

ANTIMICROBIAL Destroys or inhibits the growth of micro-organisms, such as bacteria and fungi

ANTIOXIDANT Prevents or slows the natural deterioration of cells that occurs as they age, due to oxidation

ANTIPARASITIC Another term for anthelmintic

ANTIRHEUMATIC Relieves the discomforts of rheumatic problems

ANTISCORBUTIC Acts as a remedy for scurvy

ANTISEPTIC Destroys and prevents the development of microbes

ANTISPASMODIC Prevents and eases muscular spasms

ANTITHROMBOTIC Counters the formation of blood clots

ANTITUMOR Combats the formation of tumors

ANTITUSSIVE Inhibits the cough reflex, helping to stop coughing

ANTIVIRAL Destroys or inhibits viruses

APHRODISIAC Increases or stimulates sexual desire

ASTRINGENT Constricts the blood vessels or membranes, reducing irritation, inflammation, and swelling

BILE A thick, oily fluid excreted by the liver; it helps the body to digest fats

BITTER Stimulates the appetite, promoting the secretion of saliva and gastric juices by exciting the taste buds

CARDIOTONIC Has a stimulating effect on the heart

CARMINATIVE Expels gas from the stomach and intestines and settles the digestive system

CHOLAGOGUE Promotes the secretion and flow of bile into the duodenum

COUNTER-IRRITANT Produces surface irritation of the skin to counteract more painful symptoms

DECONGESTANT Relieves or reduces congestion (e.g. mucus)

DEMULCENT Protects the mucous membranes and alleviates irritation

DEPURATIVE Helps to combat impurity in the blood

DIAPHORETIC Promotes sweating

DIURETIC Promotes urination and increases the flow

EMETIC Induces vomiting

EMMENAGOGUE Promotes menstruation

EMOLLIENT Softens and soothes the skin

ESTROGENIC Affects the hormone estrogen, which controls female sexual development, function, and secondary sexual characteristics (e.g. breast development)

EXCESS (OR *SHI*) SYNDROMES Syndromes where there is a surplus or congestion of basic constituents (i.e. *Qi*, blood, or body fluids) or inadequate function of any *Zang Fu* organs

EXPECTORANT Encourages the coughing reflex

FEBRIFUGE/FEBRIFUGAL Combats fever

GALACTAGOGUE Increases the secretion of milk

HEMOPTYSIS Coughing up blood, a symptom that should always be reported to health-care professionals

HEMOSTATIC Arrests bleeding

HEPATIC Relating to the liver

HORMONAL ACTION Promotes the production of hormones of the male or female sex organs, the adrenal cortex, pituitary, thyroid or other glands

HYPERGLYCEMIC Raises blood-sugar levels

HYPERTENSIVE Raises blood pressure

HYPOGLYCEMIC Lowers blood-sugar levels

HYPOTENSIVE Lowers blood pressure

LAXATIVE Promotes defecation

LYMPHATIC Pertaining to the lymph system

MENORRHAGIA Abnormally heavy menstrual bleeding

METABOLIC Relating to metabolism: the sum of all chemical and physical changes that take place within the body and enable its continued growth and functioning

NERVINE A herb that has some action—relaxing, stimulating, restoring, or tonifying—on the nervous system

NUTRIENT A non-irritating, easily digestible agent that provides body nourishment and stimulates the metabolism

NUTRITIVE Substance that promotes nutrition

PARTUS PRAEPARATOR Preparation for childbirth

PATHOGENIC Causing or producing disease

PEDUNCLE The stalk of a flower

PERICARDIUM The membrane surrounding the heart

PERIPHERAL VASODILATOR A substance that dilates (relaxes) certain blood vessels to help reduce raised blood pressure and increase blood flow

PERISTALSIS Rhythmic movement of the gut to push food along the intestinal tract

PHOTOSENSITIVITY A reaction to light

PITUITARY GLAND A gland located at the base of the brain that produces a number of important hormones and regulates endocrine function

PLUMULE The primary bud of a plant, from which the stem develops

PURGATIVE Stimulates evacuation of the bowels

RECEPTACLE The elongated tip of a stem, from which simple flowers arise

REJUVENATIVE Promotes feelings of youthfulness

RESTORATIVE Helps strengthen and revive the body systems

RHIZOME/RHIZOME NODE A horizontal creeping underground stem, which acts as a root or bulb and may contain nodes from which shoots arise

RUBEFACIENT Causes redness of the skin by increasing local blood supply

SALICYLATES Salts of salicylic acid; found in many foods and drugs (such as aspirin) that are generally anti-inflammatory and help to reduce fevers

SAPONINS A group of glycosides (chemicals found in plants), so named because they produce a soaplike froth in water; very similar to steroidal hormones and sometimes with an irritant action on the mucous membranes; often used as expectorants

SEDATIVE Calming, soothing

SMOOTH MUSCLE The tissue that makes up parts of the body (other than the muscles of the limbs) which involve movement (e.g. the digestive tract)

STASIS Stagnation

STEROIDAL ACTION Mimics the action of steroids (types of hormones) produced in the body; often anti-inflammatory

STROBILES Female flowers

STYPTIC An astringent agent that reduces or stops external bleeding

SYSTEMIC Affecting the body as a whole

TESTOSTEROGENIC Affects the hormone testosterone, which controls male sexual development, function, and secondary sexual characteristics

TONIC Enlivens and strengthens the whole or specific parts of the body

TOPICAL Applied externally to a part of the body

UTERINE Pertaining to the uterus

VASODILATOR A substance that dilates the blood vessels to help reduce raised blood pressure and increase blood flow

Useful addresses/further reading

Australia

Herbal organizations

NATIONAL HERBALISTS'
ASSOCIATION OF AUSTRALIA
Suite 14
247–9 Kingsgrove Road
Kingsgrove
New South Wales 2208

VICTORIA HERBALISTS'
ASSOCIATION
24 Russell Street
Northcote
Victoria 3070

Suppliers

BLACKMORES LTD
23 Roseberry Street
Balgowlah
New South Wales 2093

GREENRIDGE BOTANICALS
PO Box 1197
Toowoomba
Queensland 4350

HERBS OF GOLD
Unit 5, 102 Bath Road
Kirrawee
New South Wales 2232

MEDIHERB PTY
PO Box 713
Warwick
Queensland 4370

NATURE'S SUNSHINE
PRODUCTS OF AUSTRALIA
PO Box 196
Doonside
New South Wales 2767

PHYTO PHARMACEUTICALS
PRODUCTS
1 Liverpool Street
Ingleburn
New South Wales 2565

SOUTHERN LIGHT HERBS
PO Box 227
Maldon
Victoria 3463

UK

Herbal organizations

COLLEGE OF AYURVEDA
20 Anne's Grove
Great Linford
Milton Keynes MK14 5DR

GENERAL COUNCIL AND
REGISTER OF CONSULTANT
HERBALISTS
Marlborough House
Swanpool
Falmouth
Cornwall TR11 4HW

NATIONAL INSTITUTE OF
MEDICAL HERBALISTS
56 Longbrook Street
Exeter
Devon EX4 6AH

REGISTER OF CHINESE
HERBAL MEDICINE
19 Trinity Road
London N2 8JJ

Mail-order herb suppliers

G. BALDWIN & CO.
171–4 Walworth Road
London SE17 1RW

EAST WEST HERBS LTD
Langston Priory Mews
Kingham
Oxon OX7 6UW

GREENWAYS
(AYURVEDIC HERBS)
The Old Clinic
10 St. John's Square
Glastonbury
Somerset BA6 9LJ

HAMBLEDON HERBS
Court Farm
Milverton
Somerset TA4 1NF

NEAL'S YARD REMEDIES
26–34 Ingate Place
London SW8 3NS

Nurseries and specialist plant suppliers

CHESHIRE HERBS
Fourfields
Forest Road
Little Budworth
Tarporley
Cheshire CW6 9ES

CHILTERN SEEDS
Bortree Stile
Ulverston
Cumbria LA12 7PB

IDEN CROFT HERBS
Frittenden Road
Staplehurst
Kent TN12 0DN

POYNTZFIELD HERB NURSERY
Black Isle
By Dingwall
Ross & Cromarty IV7 8LX

USA

Herbal organizations

AMERICAN BOTANICAL
COUNCIL
PO Box 210660
Austin
TX 78720

AMERICAN HERBAL
PRODUCTS ASSOCIATION
PO Box 2410/
PO Box 210660
Austin
TX 78720

AMERICAN HERBALISTS'
GUILD
PO Box 1683
Soquel
CA 95073

HERB RESEARCH FEDERATION
1007 Pearl Street
Suite 500
Boulder
CO 808302

NORTHEAST HERB
ASSOCIATION
PO Box 266
Milton
NY 12547

Suppliers

BAY LAUREL FARM
West Garzas Road
Camel Valley
CA 93924

FRONTIER HERBS
Box 299
Norway
IO 52318

HERB PRODUCTS CO.
11012 Magnolia Blvd
North Hollywood
CA 91601

KIEHLS PHARMACY
109 Third Avenue
New York
NY 10009

MAY WAY TRADING
CHINESE HERB COMPANY
1338 Cypress Street
Oakland
CA 94607

SAGE MOUNTAIN HERBS
PO Box 420
East Barre
VT 05649

Further reading

Bartram, T., *Encyclopaedia of Herbal Medicine*, Grace Publishers, Christchurch, 1995

Bown, D., *Encyclopaedia of Herbs and Their Uses*, Dorling Kindersley, 1995

Chevallier, A., *Encyclopaedia of Medicinal Plants*, Dorling Kindersley, London, 1996

Davis, P., *Aromatherapy: An A–Z*, 2nd edition, C. W. Daniels, Saffron Walden, 1995

Foster, S., and Yue, C., *Herbal Emissaries*, Healings Arts Press, Rochester, VT, 1992

Frawley, D., *Ayurvedic Healing: A Comprehensive Guide*, Passage Press, Salt Lake City, UT, 1989

Frawley, D., and Lad, V., *The Yoga of Herbs*, Lotus Press, Santa Fe, NM, 1986

Grieve, M., *A Modern Herbal*, Jonathan Cape, London, 1931

Hobbs, C., *Medicinal Mushrooms*, Botanica Press, Santa Cruz, CA, 1995

Holmes, P., *The Energetics of Western Herbs*, Artemis Press, Boulder, CO, 1989

Kaptchuk, T., *Chinese Medicine: The Web that has no Weaver*, Rider, London, 1983

Lipp, F. J., *Herbalism*, Macmillan, London, 1996

McIntyre, A., *Herbs for Pregnancy and Childbirth*, Sheldon Press, London, 1988

Newell, C. A., Anderson, L. A., and Phillipson, J. D., *Herbal Medicines*, Pharmaecutical Press, London, 1996

Ody, P., *The Complete Medicinal Herbal*, Dorling Kindersley, London, 1993

Ody, P., *100 Great Natural Remedies*, Kyle Cathie, London, 1997

Ody, P., *Herbs for First Aid*, Keats, Los Angeles, CA, 1999

Tisserand, R., *The Art of Aromatherapy*, C. W. Daniels, Saffron Walden, 1977

Vogel, V. J., *American Indian Medicine*, University of Oklahoma Press, OK, 1970

Weiss, R. F., *Herbal Medicine*, Beaconsfield Publishers, Beaconsfield, 1988

Wren, R. C., *Potter's New Cyclopaedia of Botanical Drugs and Preparations*, C. W. Daniels, Saffron Walden, 1988

Index

Acknowledgments

Information on the energetics of Western herbs
is derived largely from the work of Peter Holmes;
on the Chinese concept of the soul in relation to
traditional therapeutics from seminars held by Ted
Kaptchuk; and on ayurvedic theory from seminars
held by Robert Svoboda and Vasant Lad. Their
understanding and learning, so generously shared,
are gratefully acknowledged.

Picture credits

The Bridgeman Art Library, London: p.20B (Victoria and Albert Museum); Getty
One/Stone, London: pp. 13T, 35T, 37T, 61T, 74B, 99B, 100T, 145B, 159T.

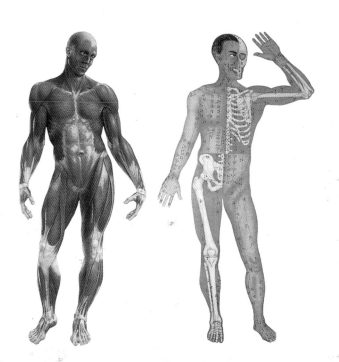